Early Praise for
CORPORATE BULLSH*T

"Stories are powerful; they shape our thinking, limit or inspire our imagination, and speed up or slow down our response to challenges. In *Corporate Bullsh*t*, Hanauer, Walsh, and Cohen expose six of the most powerful—and bogus—stories corporations have relied on to keep us from challenging their abuses. The first step in real progress is exposing and dismantling these stories and *Corporate Bullsh*t* does exactly that."

—Ann Leonard, creator of *The Story of Stuff* and former director of Greenpeace USA

"It would be hilarious if it wasn't so sad: *Corporate Bullsh*t* traces how the wealthy and powerful have used the same tired excuses for centuries, to defend outrages from slavery to coal-mining deaths to unequal pay for women, through the current deadly threat of fossil-fueled climate disaster. The examples will make you laugh and make you angry—and then make you act!"

—Lizz Winstead, co-creator of *The Daily Show*

"Most decent people intuitively know when they're being lied to by corporate America. We get that their narratives are propaganda deployed to line their own pockets. But we don't always understand how. *Corporate Bullsh*t* exposes the nuggets of lies at the core of their stories. It pulls back the asterisk to reveal the word we knew was there all along."

—Elie Mystal, author of *Allow Me to Retort: A Black Guy's Guide to the Constitution*

"*Corporate Bullsh*t* fights against the way the power elite has co-opted the so-called 'American way,' when so many of its priorities—unchecked corporate power, the suppression of equal rights for women and people of color, and the defunding of American institutions from labor protections to education equality—are really un-American. Read it, and fight."

—Svante Myrick, president of People for the American Way

"As an elected official, I hear these lies from corporate special interests all the time: Raising taxes on the rich will kill jobs, raising the minimum wage will hurt the very people it's intended to help, and regulation will destroy business. None of them are true, but they're carefully crafted to trick working people into prioritizing corporate interests over their own. *Corporate Bullsh*t* pulls back the curtain on their game plan and makes a compelling argument for reforms to grow America from the bottom up and the middle out."

—Congresswoman Pramila Jayapal

"This book is not only a crucial tool to combat more than a century of corporate disinformation—it's a rollicking good read that will have you laughing out loud as you learn how to rout it and win. Get a copy into the hands of everyone you know so we don't get fooled again. Even your cranky uncle could change his mind."

—Nancy MacLean, author of *Democracy in Chains: The Deep History of the Radical Right's Stealth Plan for America*

"Whether it's 1923 or 2023, the same trickle-down nonsense used in every boardroom in America hasn't changed. This book pulls back the curtain on the whole racket in a way that leaves you unsure whether to laugh or cry, but sure of one thing: It's not true. It's never been true."

—Ben Cohen, co-founder, Ben & Jerry's

CORPORATE BULLSH*T

CORPORATE

BULLSH*T

EXPOSING THE LIES AND HALF-TRUTHS
THAT PROTECT PROFIT, POWER, AND WEALTH IN AMERICA

NICK HANAUER, JOAN WALSH, AND DONALD COHEN

THE
NEW
PRESS

NEW YORK
LONDON

Requests for permission to reproduce selections from this book should
be made through our website: https://thenewpress.com/contact.

Published in the United States by The New Press, New York, 2023
Distributed by Two Rivers Distribution

LIBRARY OF CONGRESS CATALOGING-IN-PUBLICATION DATA

Names: Hanauer, Nick, author. | Walsh, Joan, 1958- author. | Cohen, Donald
(Public interest advocate), author.
Title: Corporate bullsh*t : exposing the lies and half-truths that protect
profit, power, and wealth in America / Nick Hanauer, Joan Walsh, and
Donald Cohen.
Other titles: Corporate bullshit
Description: New York : The New Press, [2023] | Includes bibliographical
references. | Summary: "An illustrated guide to decoding decades of free
market hypocrisy and deception"-- Provided by publisher.
Identifiers: LCCN 2023016522 | ISBN 9781620977514 (board) | ISBN
9781620977729 (ebook)
Subjects: LCSH: Corporations--Moral and ethical aspects--United States. |
Corporate power--United States. | Corporate governance--United States. |
Capitalism--Moral and ethical aspects--United States.
Classification: LCC HD2785 .H29 2023 | DDC 174/.4--dc23/eng/20230407
LC record available at https://lccn.loc.gov/2023016522

The New Press publishes books that promote and enrich public discussion and understanding
of the issues vital to our democracy and to a more equitable world. These books are made possible
by the enthusiasm of our readers; the support of a committed group of donors, large and small;
the collaboration of our many partners in the independent media and the not-for-profit sector;
booksellers, who often hand-sell New Press books; librarians; and above all by our authors.

www.thenewpress.com

Book design and composition by Bookbright Media
This book was set in Wolfgang, Barlet, and Florensans

Printed in the United States of America

2 4 6 8 10 9 7 5 3 1

CONTENTS

PREFACE—DEFENDING THE INDEFENSIBLE
HOW THE RICH AND POWERFUL PROTECT THEIR INTERESTS

NICK HANAUER

FEW ISSUES HAVE MOVED MORE QUICKLY FROM FRINGE to consensus than the Fight for $15. When colleagues and I suggested at a Democratic political conference in early November 2012 that we should raise the minimum wage to $15 an hour, people in the audience literally laughed. When New York City fast-food workers first walked off the job two weeks later demanding a $15 minimum wage (more than twice the federal rate of $7.25, both then and now), the number was widely dismissed as overreaching and symbolic—a mere bargaining tactic on the part of workers who had little if any bargaining power at all. Nobody predicted what would follow. As an early and vocal advocate for $15, even I was surprised by how fast public opinion would fall in line.

But as remarkable as this political progress has been, the political rhetoric surrounding the minimum wage remains surprisingly unchanged. Minimum wage opponents continue to deride every proposed increase as a surefire job killer, while reporters and pundits reliably characterize the passage of every minimum wage ordinance and statute as a dangerous experiment that threatens to harm the very people it's intended to help. "California makes itself a guinea pig in a massive and risky minimum wage experiment" tweeted the *New York Times*'s Noam Scheiber. "Raising minimum wage risky," the *Lexington Herald-Leader*'s letter-to-the-editor headline tersely warned its Kentucky readers following $15 victories in faraway California and New York. "Raising minimum wage hurts low-skill workers," the *Detroit News* bluntly chimed in. "Even left-leaning economists say it's a gamble," *Vox* solemnly cautioned (without actually managing to cite a single left-leaning economist willing to pejoratively editorialize $15 as a "gamble").

The confidence of the doomsayers and the anxiety of the pundits might make more sense if they hadn't been making the same dire predictions since before the federal minimum wage was passed in 1938—or if at least some of these dire predictions had actually come true. In fact, contrary to the cautionary headlines, there is nothing "experimental" about raising the minimum wage. The federal minimum wage has been raised 22 times since it was first established—state and local minimum wages have been raised hundreds of times—yet study after peer-reviewed study has found little or no correlation between the minimum wage and levels of employment. So why do opponents continue to make the same bullshit, baseless claims over and over again?

Because *they work*.

Over the past century and a half, on a broad range of issues including the minimum wage, paid overtime, workplace safety, environmental regulations, consumer protection—even on morally indisputable issues like child labor and racial segregation—the people and corporations who profited from the status quo have effectively wielded a familiar litany of groundless "economic" claims and fearmongering rhetoric in their efforts to slow or quash necessary reforms. As even a cursory examination of the quotes we've included in this book will show, the wealthy and powerful are willing to say anything—even the worst things imaginable—to retain their wealth and power. But while there is simply no bottom to this well of shamelessness, *there is a pattern*.

This book is an exposé of the people and corporations that defend the indefensible, and the predictable patterns of lies and half-truths—in other words, the bullshit—they use to protect their profit, power, and wealth. Our hope is that by revealing these patterns, you and millions like you can more easily recognize and reject the corporate bullshit that has long dominated our public debates.

I've had an insider's view from both sides of this fight. As a venture capitalist and serial entrepreneur who has founded, co-founded, and funded more than 30 companies across a range of industries, I've sat in some of the corporate suites and boardrooms from which anti-reform money and propaganda flow. As the founder of Civic Ventures, a Seattle-based public policy incubator that's been on the front lines of campaigns to boost the minimum wage, paid over-time, paid leave, secure scheduling, and other impor-tant reforms, I've found myself endlessly refuting the same undying corporate lies, over and over and over.

The acts of corporate lies and malfeasance docu-mented in this book are so prevalent and so mun-danely audacious that we often fail to recognize them for what they are: threats masquerading as economic theory. They are always some variation on the same familiar themes: "If you raise the cost of labor, employers will purchase less of it," we've been warned. "If you raise taxes on the wealthy, they'll have less money to invest in creating good-paying jobs." If you regulate this or that unsafe workplace practice, make products less toxic, the environment less polluted, the poor less poor, or investors less rich, "you'll only end up hurting the very people you are trying to help." It's a narrative grounded in credulous concern-trolling—an economic "theory" wrapped around a protection racket for the superrich: "Nice economy you have there," we are warned. "It would be a shame if anything were to happen to it."

These threats fall neatly into what is commonly known as "trickle-down economics." It's not really economics in any scientific sense. It is simply a time-tested way for the powerful to assert control over the less powerful. For the real magic of trickle-down eco-nomics isn't convincing you that if the rich get richer, that's good for the economy. The real power comes from convincing you that if the poor get richer, that would be bad *for the poor*. It is a clever catch-22: Low wages and long hours may trap you and your children in a vicious circle of poverty, but they are the only things that guarantee you a job at all.

What I learned from the Fight for $15 isn't that the trickle-downers feared it would raise wages for near-ly half of Americans (although it would certainly do that). Rather, they feared that it would expose trickle-down economics for what it truly is—an intimida-tion tactic, a con job, a scam—a rhetorical negotiating strategy that has been deftly used to pick the pock-ets of American workers for the past 40 years. The opponents of reform aren't afraid they will harm the economy. They are terrified these reforms will help the economy, and by so doing, demolish the lies that rationalize the current regime of economic policies that empower and enrich them.

*Corporate Bullsh*t* aims to make these lies more vis-ible, and by so doing, inoculate readers against the harmful and insidious narratives that continue to muddy the public debate. By seeing these arguments in the context of history, we can clearly understand them for what they are: antisocial lies cloaked in pro-social narratives. We do not have to believe or repeat these bullshit lies any longer.

Today, in spite of all of the evidence to the contrary, powerful interests continue to argue that raising wages for workers is bad for workers, that raising tax rates on corporations or on the rich will kill jobs and productivity, that climate change isn't real, and that addressing it will make us all poor. They argue that the way to make us safer from gun violence is to sell more guns, and that reforming our healthcare system will make us poorer and sicker. They warn that nearly everything the people want and the powerful oppose is "socialism." And so on.

Mountains of evidence have not yet persuaded the rich and powerful to stop defending their power and wealth. That's why refuting these claims is never enough. Mere refutation is like bringing a knife to a gunfight. We must go beyond refutation and instead use what the powerful fear most: shame, ridicule, and moral censure. We must hold people who create harm in our society accountable, and we must use political power to require the powerful to act in prosocial ways. We cannot do that if we are confused about corporate intentions or tricked by these narratives.

When most people recognize these claims for what they are—con jobs, intimidation tactics, malfeasance, and lies—the power of these claims is diminished and our ability as citizens to build a more just, prosperous, and sustainable future is enhanced. This is the purpose of this book. It is our hope that by reading it, you will never be fooled, conned, intimidated, or bamboozled by the powerful again.

INTRODUCTION

Cartoon by Barry Deutsch.

IT'S A FIGHT THAT'S BEEN GOING ON FOR CENTURIES—and it continues to this day.

From the movement to abolish slavery to the campaign to end child labor; from the Progressive Era push for a fairer tax system to the decades-long quest to create and then strengthen the social safety net; from the effort to protect lives from dangerous cars and chemicals to today's urgent struggle to curb climate change—much of our history has been a battle between ordinary Americans mobilizing to build a fairer, safer, stronger country, and political or corporate elites resisting reform in order to preserve a skewed status quo that serves their interests. These elites rely on a set of lies that they've recycled, sometimes for decades, sometimes longer. Again and again, industries deny problems—smoking doesn't cause cancer; cars don't cause pollution; greedy pharmaceutical companies aren't responsible for the crisis of opioid addiction—long after evidence to the contrary is widely available.

Regular people have won plenty of victories. The core of the New Deal, which created the foundations of social support and economic opportunity we rely on today, has endured for nearly a century thanks to a popular movement that has rallied support behind it. Far fewer Americans die on the roads than used to be the case, because we required automakers to build safer cars. Fewer workers are injured, sickened, or killed on the job thanks to workplace safety regulations, and minimum wage laws mean more workers are economically secure. Our kids breathe cleaner air and drink cleaner water than our parents and grandparents did. We've dramatically cut poverty, especially among the elderly, and steadily expanded access to healthcare. We've made it much harder for businesses or the government to single out women, people of color, and LGBTQ Americans for unfair treatment.

But every advance has been a struggle, and waves of progress have often been followed by periods in which the forces of power and privilege have reasserted control. In the decades after the New Deal and World War II, the United States created an infrastructure of opportunity that built the world's largest middle class and broadly shared the gains of a long economic boom. Of course, given our country's despicable history of racism, systemic exclusion, and institutional oppression, communities of color, including Black, Indigenous, and Hispanic Americans were and continue to be largely left out of this prosperity, often by design. For white Americans, the economy during this period was characterized by a striking degree of equality. In the years from 1947 to 1973, under presidents of both parties, real wages rose by 81 percent, while wages for the top 1 percent rose by less than half of that.

By the 1970s, though, corporations and their political allies began to organize aggressively to restore their supremacy. They funded a cadre of "think tanks," university programs, advocacy groups, and media organizations to flip the script and portray "big government" as the villain and themselves as the true victims. "The federal government fought a war on poverty, and poverty won," President Ronald Reagan intoned in 1981, influentially but wrongly, as he began weakening the nation's investments in New Deal policies that for decades had leveled the playing field between corporations and consumers, owners and employees, the very wealthy and the rest of us.

Today, the income and wealth gaps that narrowed after World War II have widened again. Income inequality increased by 20 percent between 1980 and 2016, according to Pew Research. The top 1 percent's share of taxable income has surged from 9 percent in 1975, to 22 percent in 2018; the bottom 90 percent have seen their income share fall, from 67 percent to 50 percent. A RAND Corporation study found that a stunning $50 trillion in wealth had been distributed upward, away from the paychecks of the bottom 90 percent of families, between 1975 and 2020, due to tax policies favoring the wealthy and wage stagnation among the non-rich. Racial wealth gaps are particularly staggering. The net worth of a typical white family is 10 times that of Black families, and in 2019, the median wealth of a Latino household was 9 percent of the median white household's wealth.

In order to redistribute wealth upward, powerful corporate elites have waged an alarmingly successful campaign to establish the terms of the economic debate with a set of now-familiar edicts: The free market knows best and should be left to do its thing; all government regulation is creeping socialism; programs like welfare and the minimum wage tend to

hurt, not help, those they aim to benefit. Many of these nostrums weren't new even decades ago. They were dusted off from the centuries-long tradition of rhetoric used by corporate and political elites to fight off reform.

Some of these lies are, frankly, too absurd to take seriously. "Ensuring seniors have healthcare will inevitably lead to communism." "Global warming is great for the planet!" You get the idea. But most are a little different. Most have been effective because, at least on the surface, they offer a civic-minded, reasonable-sounding justification for positions that in fact are motivated entirely by self-interest. "We'd love to pay our workers a living wage, but then we'd have to lay people off, which no one wants!" "We really want to build safer cars, so it's best if you just leave us alone to do it instead of requiring it." And so on. It doesn't matter much if the argument holds up under scrutiny—just by existing, these false claims can suggest the existence of a good-faith debate. Once that happens, most people don't have time to figure out who's right.

As Americans try to fight their way through this blizzard of lies, it can help to notice that myriad falsehoods can be categorized into some common, overlapping stories. False stories, fake stories, but sometimes beguiling stories nonetheless. Soothing but toxic fairy tales.

This book identifies the Big Six:

It's Not A Problem! The first step is denial. For whatever harmful practice they want to defend, from slavery to smoking to global pollution, defenders of the status quo simply say the problems don't exist, or are overblown, or that we don't really know for sure. Sometimes they go further, claiming that it's not just not a problem, it's actually a good thing.

When finally forced to admit a problem, they default to a few reliable comebacks. One favorite: **The Free Market Can Fix It!** Sure, sometimes . . . *stuff* happens. But our free enterprise system ensures that businesses will make things right. No need for worker safety laws, since "safety is good business," the U.S. Chamber of Commerce told Congress in 1973. Civil rights laws applied to private business? No need! Patrons would put places that discriminated out of business. (Spoiler alert: In the Jim Crow South, those places flourished.)

Or, they say **It's Not Our Fault—It's Your Fault!** On-the-job injuries? Blame it on worker carelessness. Consumer safety issues? All about lazy, bargain-hunting consumers. The 2008 housing crash? The fault of greedy people who wanted homes they couldn't afford and do-gooder advocates who forced banks to make loans to people who didn't deserve them.

If reform efforts begin to gain traction, they focus on what they say would be the catastrophic consequences of actually taking action to fix the problem. For instance: **It's a Job Killer!** From the earliest efforts to improve workplace safety and pay levels, going back to the nineteenth century, industry leaders have lamented, insisted, threatened, or howled that any proposal will wind up costing jobs and tanking the economy. Public health and environmental protections that we today take for granted would have killed whole industries by now if the wolf-crying opponents had been correct.

Here's a related objection: **You'll Only Make Things Worse!** Trying to fix the problem, they warn, will backfire, bringing unintended consequences that often hurt the people you're trying to help. Welfare hurts the poor. The minimum wage is bad for workers. Women's suffrage will lure women out of the home, meaning men won't like them anymore—and children will die! And so on.

If all else fails there's the old reliable: **It's Socialism!** As you'll see, every president going back to FDR who has pushed for a fairer society has been trashed as a socialist, or at the very least, a dupe imposing a socialist agenda driven by others. Likewise, almost any major effort to protect workers or the public from dangerous, dirty, or unhealthy products or practices has earned the socialist label.

But times are changing. The 2008 financial crash and the Great Recession that followed, not to mention the existential threat of climate change, have permanently and fundamentally undermined the notion that corporations and the free market can be left to regulate themselves. A series of massive corporate tax cuts has done little to spur jobs and broad-based growth, discrediting trickle-down economics. Meanwhile, decades-long economic inequality and the COVID-19 pandemic have exposed a badly frayed safety net. It's now clearer than ever that these arguments—some advanced by corporations and their allies for over a century—almost never held water. Over and over, the disasters they predicted somehow never came to pass.

All of this has ignited a new movement for a government that does more to level the playing field and ensure everyone has a chance to prosper—one that can update the New Deal and the Great Society for the twenty-first century. For that movement to succeed, we need to bury these lies once and for all. To do that, we need to understand how they work: how the same clever-sounding myths that have been hammered into our heads almost since the Founding are constantly updated and recycled; how they use denial, uncertainty, blame-shifting, and a phony pose of civic responsibility; and how they have almost always been proven false by reality.

The stakes couldn't be higher. Building a fairer, stronger country is urgent for its own sake. At a time when our democracy is under assault, it may also be the only way to restore faith that our system can still respond to big problems and improve Americans' lives in concrete ways.

If we can see through these howlers once and for all, we can rob them of the power they've held for much too long to shape public opinion. Once that happens, we can start building a country that truly provides a fair chance for everyone.

CHAPTER 1

IT'S NOT
A PROBLEM

It is but the natural course of mining events that men should be injured and killed by accidents.

Gov. G. W. Atkinson of West Virginia, 1901

There is absolutely no proof that cigarettes are addictive.

Edward Horrigan, R. J. Reynolds CEO, 1982

I'm in Los Angeles and it's freezing. Global warming is a total, and very expensive, hoax!

Donald Trump, 2013

THE REACTION OF CORPORATE INTERESTS TO THE LEGITIMATE DEMANDS OF ORDINARY AMERICANS ALMOST ALWAYS begins with denial. Shameless denial. As social reformers marshal their arguments, whether against slavery, climate change, smoking dangers, or pay inequities, some version of the petulant cry *"It's not a problem!"* always rings from the other side as they scheme to protect their power and profits.

Often, it involves casting doubt on scientific or technical findings to prevent the public from recognizing that an expert consensus has emerged. And frequently these false claims come with ludicrous arguments: Grade-school-aged kids forced to work in mines and mills are happy and healthy! Toxic pollution in our air and water might seem problematic, but it's fine. True, we've had decades' worth of studies showing that smoking is dangerous, but we really don't know for sure, so why worry?

Sometimes they go further still: Slavery, child labor, and climate change, according to their defenders, aren't just *Not a Problem*—they're actually good things that bring benefits for everyone!

Over time, reformers have won many of these battles. But that doesn't stop the forces of wealth and power from using the same denials time and again. One reason this lie is so effective is that it challenges the reformers' very first premise—that the problem exists at all. By bogging them down in having to first prove that lead is bad for kids or smoking kills, the lie makes it that much harder to get to a place where we're discussing solutions.

And remember, this denial isn't just a dishonest rhetorical strategy. It has grave, real-world consequences, often measured in deaths or serious illnesses. They ought to be ashamed—but then, many are shameless. They're making too much money doing the wrong thing.

NEVER BEFORE HAS THE BLACK RACE OF CENTRAL AFRICA, FROM THE DAWN OF HISTORY TO THE PRESENT DAY, ATTAINED A CONDITION SO *civilized* AND SO *improved*, NOT ONLY PHYSICALLY, BUT MORALLY AND INTELLECTUALLY.
—JOHN CALHOUN, 1837

Distortions like these go back to the shame of slavery. As the abolition movement spread, and more Americans came to understand slavery's cruelty and injustice, its political and economic defenders began not merely denying slavery was a problem, but delusionally claiming that it was in fact a positive good—including for the enslaved.

> *As a class, I say it boldly; there is not a happier, more contented race upon the face of the earth. . . . Lightly tasked, well clothed, well fed—far better than the free laborers of any country in the world . . . their lives and persons protected by the law, all their sufferings alleviated by the kindest and most interested care.*
>
> Rep. James Henry Hammond of South Carolina, 1836

> *Never before has the black race of Central Africa, from the dawn of history to the present day, attained a condition so civilized and so improved, not only physically, but morally and intellectually. . . . It came to us in a low, degraded, and savage condition, and in the course*

of a few generations it has grown up under the fostering care of our institutions.

Sen. and former Vice President
John Calhoun of South Carolina, 1837

The negro slaves of the South are the happiest, and, in some sense, the freest people in the world. The children and the aged and infirm work not at all, and yet have all the comforts and necessaries of life provided for them. They enjoy liberty, because they are oppressed neither by care nor labor. The women do little hard work, and are protected from the despotism of their husbands by their masters.

George Fitzhugh,
prominent pro-slavery theorist, 1857

Just as the enslaved were—in the eyes of the rich and powerful—happy, so were child laborers. As far back as 1791, Alexander Hamilton, every Broadway musical fan's favorite founder, argued that children "who would otherwise be idle" could be a source of cheap labor in the manufacturing future he envisioned for his young country. In 1900, an estimated 18 percent of children between the ages of 10 and 15, most of whose families lived in poverty, were employed, increasingly in unsafe factory or mining jobs. By then, Progressive reformers had begun to fight the practice. Industry defenders fought back, however, arguing that those opposed to child labor just didn't know how good these kids had it. In other words, *It's Not a Problem* . . .

I have seen children working in factories, and I have seen them working at home and they were perfectly happy.

Mabel A. Clark, canning company executive, 1913

We do not ourselves approve of the glass house or the cotton mill for ungrown youths, and we believe that no unhealthy occupation should be followed till a period of robustness and physical resistance is reached. But the mine is healthy. We have proof of it, in the hardiness of its workers, their muscular development and their longevity.

Coal Age, the leading coal industry journal, 1912

I HAVE SEEN *children* WORKING IN FACTORIES, AND I HAVE SEEN THEM WORKING AT HOME AND THEY WERE PERFECTLY *happy.*
—MABEL A. CLARK, 1913

The pictures which your committee has published as representative of conditions in the Southern textile mills show thin, emaciated children that look too weak to stand. But I am willing to wager that the children in the mill district, boy for boy, can lick any other class of boys in America.

David Clark, *Southern Textile Bulletin* editor, 1915

Still, a growing number of states were restricting child labor and seeing clear benefits. In the 1920s, for the first time, a near majority of high school-age students remained in school—an eightfold increase in high school enrollments since 1900. But federal efforts to limit child labor were thwarted by the U.S. Supreme Court, which had twice in recent years struck down as unconstitutional laws restricting work by minors. That led Congress in 1924 to pass a constitutional amendment giving itself the authority to regulate child labor. In response, industry and its backers launched a furious campaign to urge states not to ratify the measure.

Our investigations thus far have indicated that the home and farm work done by the average farm boy or girl is well balanced with other activities, and is much preferable to the loafing leisure and trouble-finding time of the city boy or girl.

Walter Burr, sociology professor at
Kansas State Agricultural College, 1924

The opposition campaign succeeded, and the amendment fell short of the number of states needed to become law. Child labor in the United States would not be banned until 1938.

But this isn't a settled issue. As of 2023, lawmakers in more than twenty states are promoting legislation that rolls back child labor protections. Here's how one governor justified signing a new law that allows children as young as fourteen years old to legally work long hours in dangerous factories and slaughterhouses:

In Iowa, we understand there is dignity in work and we pride ourselves on our strong work ethic. Instilling those values in the next generation and providing opportunities for young adults to earn and save to build a better life should be available.

Gov. Kim Reynolds of Iowa, 2023

Just as slavery and child labor were *Not a Problem* in the eyes of their defenders, dangerous and dirty working conditions that led to unsanitary, even tainted, food and other products were also nothing to worry about.

DENIES CHILD LABOR TALES.

Southern Editor Tells Reformers to Mind Their Own Business.

Special to The New York Times.

WASHINGTON, Jan. 6.—Denial that children are oppressed and overworked in the mills of North Carolina was made by David Clark, editor of The Southern Textile Bulletin, at the session of the National Child Labor Committee today. Mr. Clark appeared and demanded to be heard, and then read a paper contradicting the statements that have been made about conditions in his State.

The session was very warm by reason of the editor's attack on the child labor workers. He was listened to attentively by the delegates. After he concluded Owen R. Lovejoy of New York, National Secretary, said that the committee was incorporated and could be held responsible for any statement about the child labor conditions in North Carolina. He added that no action had been started against the committee by any of the mill owners concerned.

"The pictures which your committee has published as representative of conditions in the Southern textile mills show thin, emaciated children that look too weak to stand," said Mr. Clark. "But I am willing to wager that the children in the mill district, boy for boy, can lick any other class of boys in America.

"They seem to have the recognized boyish proclivity for getting into trouble and doing things they ought not to do. I will agree to get any member of this committee a position in a North Carolina textile mill where they will have charge of these boys, and if at the end of two weeks you still retain your sanity you must agree that these boys are anything but vitiated.

"I have never seen a statement issued by the Child Labor Committee that did not exaggerate conditions and tell half truths. They take isolated cases and create the impression that they are representative. Furthermore, the fact that a boy of 13 years works in North Carolina can in no way injure citizens of New York and Massachusetts, and, plainly speaking, it is none of their business."

Senator Owen said that the only way to protect children against harsh treatment was through the interstate commerce powers of the Federal Government. He said that in many States the Legislatures were frequently controlled by bi-partisan machines, and therefore an adequate child labor law could not be obtained by State enactment. He declared that both the States and the nation had a duty to perform, and that the national welfare required action by the Federal Government. For that reason Mr. Owen said that he favored the Palmer-Owen bill prohibiting the shipment of any articles in interstate commerce made by child labor.

January 7, 1915. Southern employers were the most opposed to child labor laws—though they had some help from Northern plutocrats.

Upton Sinclair's best-selling 1906 novel, *The Jungle*, serialized the year before in magazines, introduced Americans to the cruelty, danger, and stomach-turning filth of the meatpacking industry. The publicity added momentum to the push for the Federal Meat Inspection Act of 1906. But industry saw no need for it.

> *It makes business sense to have them clean. We want them to be sanitary, and expect them to be sanitary, and will do anything in reason to make them sanitary.*
>
> Thomas Wilson, meatpacking industry spokesman, 1906

> *Meat canned five years ago is just as good as meat canned six months ago. . . . Of course [putting the date on a can] benefits nobody if the meat is just as good with age, like whisky is said to be, as it is without.*
>
> Judge Samuel H. Cowan,
> attorney for the Texas Cattle Raisers Association and the
> American National Live Stock Association, 1906

Dangerous conditions in cotton mills?

> *It's rather asinine to think cotton fiber is hazardous. There's no evidence of that. . . . Breathing cotton dust fiber is like breathing carrot juice—it doesn't feel good but it won't hurt you.*
>
> Gov. Ray Blanton of Tennessee, 1978

OF COURSE [PUTTING THE DATE ON A CAN] BENEFITS *nobody* IF THE MEAT IS JUST AS GOOD WITH AGE, LIKE WHISKY IS SAID TO BE, AS IT IS WITHOUT. –JUDGE SAMUEL H. COWAN, 1906

The very same article in the *Sarasota Herald-Tribune* that quoted Governor Blanton included reporting that inhalation of "[cotton] dust has been linked to byssinnosis [sic], or brown lung disease—a respiratory illness found among textile workers," but that the "[textile] industry has contended that the new standards are too costly and are impossible to implement," referring to the Occupational Safety and Health Administration's newly implemented regulations to "reduce cotton dust by about 80 percent in textile plants."

Air and water pollution? That's fine too.

> *Industrial waste is not a menace to public health . . . it is sewage which does the harm.*
>
> E. W. Tinker, American Paper and Pulp Association, 1947

> *The water that comes out of our plants . . . in many cases . . . is purer than the water that came from the river before we used it.*
>
> Irving Shapiro, Du Pont Chemical Co. chair, 1981

Same for cars—both in terms of pollution and safety:

> *The Ford engineering staff, although mindful that automobile engines produce exhaust gases, feel these waste vapors are dissipated in the atmosphere quickly and do not present an air pollution problem.*
>
> Dan J. Chabek, Ford Motor Co., 1953

November 14, 1976. A Herblock Cartoon, © The Herb Block Foundation.

There is no scientific evidence showing a threat to health from automotive emissions in the normal, average air you breathe. Not even in crowded cities.

Chrysler ad, 1972

Shoulder harnesses [seat belts] and head rests are complete wastes of money.

Lee Iacocca, Chrysler chairman, 1971

And drug safety:

[There is] still no positive proof of a causal relationship between the use of thalidomide during pregnancy and malformations in the newborn.

John. N. Premi, M.D., Medical Director of William S. Merrell Co., maker of thalidomide, 1962

Appeal to the doctor's ego—we think he is important enough to be selected as one of the first to use Kevadon in that section of the country. . . . Bear in mind that these are not basic clinical research studies. We have firmly established the safety, dosage, and usefulness of Kevadon by both foreign and U.S. laboratory and clinical studies.

William S. Merrell Co., Kevadon (brand name for thalidomide) marketing document obtained by the FDA, 1962

By 1962, "10,000 children, mostly in Europe, had been born with thalidomide-induced birth defects." In a rare defeat for drug companies, the Food and Drug Administration refused to approve thalidomide for use by pregnant women, thanks in large part to one conscientious medical officer, Dr. Frances Kelsey, who stood up to industry pressure and demanded more tests after seeing something odd in the drugs' trials. As a result, the American impact was much less severe.

Race- and gender-based pay inequalities, likewise, were nothing to worry about:

> Even if it [the Equal Pay Act] could be administered and enforced, no evidence is presented demonstrating a need for it.
>
> Norman J. Simler,
> White House Council of Economic Advisers, 1963

And neither was the fact that some workers aren't paid enough to get by, since that never happens:

> Emotional appeals about working families trying to get by on $4.25 an hour are hard to resist. Fortunately, such families don't really exist.
>
> Rep. Tom DeLay of Texas, 1996

SHOULDER HARNESSES [SEAT BELTS] AND HEAD RESTS ARE *complete wastes of money.*
–LEE IACOCCA, 1971

PESTICIDES DEFENDED

Public Is Said to Have Protection from Hazards at Misuse

L. S. Hitchner, Executive Secretary, National Agricultural Chemical Association, The New York Times, August 16, 1961

And don't forget pesticides:

> *There have been no reports of illness or death which can be attributed to pesticides when they were properly used and the precautions followed.*
>
> D. Lyle Goleman,
> Ohio Agricultural Research and Development Center, 1971

> *We are disappointed that they have chosen to continue to insist there is peril in fruits and vegetables. The risks are remote and hypothetical.*
> John McClung, United Fresh Fruit and Vegetable Association, 1999

Lead, whether in paint, gasoline, or anywhere else, also never did anyone any harm:

> *Lead helps to guard your health.*
> National Lead Company ad, 1923

> *There is no evidence that lead in the atmosphere, from autos or any other source, poses a health hazard.*
> John Kimberley, Lead Industries Association, 1970

For over 50 years, the National Lead Company preached the fictional safety of lead, even for children, with its "Dutch Boy" ads. Courtesy the Winterthur Library: Printed Book and Periodical Collection.

> *The people in this room have the same amount of lead in their blood*
> *as do the natives in New Guinea. If you take lead out of the air, you'll*
> *still have it in your body.*
>
> Dr. George Rausch, Tulane University professor, 1971

In fact, lead, which irrevocably damages children's brains, is estimated to cause at least 674,000 deaths worldwide and cost almost $1 trillion, per year. The worldwide drive by the United Nations to stop using leaded gasoline is projected to prevent more than 1.2 million premature deaths. But after seventy years of denial (and lots of lives lost), the people finally won. In July of 2008, Congress passed legislation banning lead in toys.

THERE
IS NO EVIDENCE
THAT LEAD IN THE
ATMOSPHERE, FROM AUTOS
OR ANY OTHER SOURCE,
POSES A *health hazard.*
–JOHN KIMBERLEY, 1970

Just as toxic pollution and unsafe working conditions never did anyone any harm, Wall Street's increasingly complex financial instruments are also totally benign, according to industry leaders.

After a wave of financial deregulation around the turn of the century, investment banks developed an alphabet soup of new and exotic financial products—mortgage-backed securities (MBSs), collateralized debt obligations (CDOs), credit default swaps (CDSs), and more.

Profits skyrocketed. In the early 2000s, Wall Street profits made up a record 40 percent of all U.S. domestic corporate profits. In 2005, around the height of the housing boom, Goldman Sachs, Bear Stearns, Lehman Brothers, and other firms raked in record profits, while financial industry bonuses hit a record $21.5 billion, with thousands receiving bonuses of $1 million or more. Reporting on the bonuses, the *New York Times*

Bush Signs Bill Banning Lead from Toys

NBC NEWS, AUGUST 14, 2008

noted: "Multimillion-dollar estates, rare art, luxury cars and fractional shares in private jets are among the more popular items coveted by Wall Street's masters of the universe."

But watch dogs were pointing out that these complex new products typically had little past performance record to use for managing risk. That meant many firms were badly exposed to any potential slump in the housing market, which could destroy the value of these assets.

Still, throughout that time, policymakers didn't see a problem.

> *Overall, the household sector seems to be in good shape, and much of the apparent increase in the household sector's debt ratios over the past decade reflects factors that do not suggest increasing household financial stress.*
>
> Federal Reserve chair Alan Greenspan, 2004

> *Although we certainly cannot rule out home price declines, especially in some local markets, these declines, were they to occur, likely would not have substantial macroeconomic implications.*
>
> Alan Greenspan, 2005

Even once it was clear the housing market was tanking, Wall Street execs and top policymakers—many of whom were uncomfortably close with each other—saw no cause for concern.

> I'M NOT AN ECONOMIST, BUT MY HOPE IS THAT THE MARKET, IF IT FUNCTIONS NORMALLY, WILL BE ABLE TO YIELD A *soft landing.*
> —PRESIDENT GEORGE W. BUSH, 2007

> *I don't see [subprime mortgage market troubles] imposing a serious problem. I think it's going to be largely contained.*
>
> Treasury Secretary and former Goldman Sachs CEO Henry Paulson, 2007

In terms of looking at housing, most of us believe that it's at or near the bottom. . . . I haven't seen a single thing that surprises me—it's hard to surprise me."

Henry Paulson, 2007

(Paulson's 2005 compensation package as Goldman CEO, FYI: $38 million).

President George W. Bush listened to his treasury secretary:

I'm not an economist, but my hope is that the market, if it functions normally, will be able to yield a soft landing. That's kind of what it looks like so far.

George W. Bush, 2007

Bush: "Soft Landing" for Markets
He Expects Investors to Calm Down and Share His Optimism About the Economy's Soundness

TAMPA BAY TIMES, AUGUST 9, 2007

The worst is likely behind us.

Paulson, May 2008

Of course, we all know what happened next. In September 2008, the collapse of Lehman Brothers triggered an economic crash that cost taxpayers trillions, and saw nearly nine million people lose their jobs and at least 10 million lose their homes. Thirteen months after the crash, the unemployment rate reached 10 percent, with many out of work for half a year or more. In some respects, the economy still hasn't recovered.

THANK YOU FOR SMOKING

In 1956—a time when nearly half of all American adults smoked—a Surgeon General's study group found that excessive smoking can cause lung cancer. In the decades that followed, the research showing smoking's myriad health risks—including emphysema, pregnancy problems, and addiction—accelerated, as did a vital public movement to restrict and discourage the habit.

For almost as long as there have been warnings about the dangers of smoking, however, there's also been a coordinated tobacco industry public relations campaign to assure people there's nothing to worry about.

At times, industry execs have argued that whatever health risks may exist, it's a personal choice:

> People in this country have a right to make up their minds. I choose to eat eggs, and drink milk, and eat cheese. And yet I have been warned about that. I think all of it tells us that research has to be done.
>
> James Bowling, Philip Morris tobacco company, 1973

The New York Times, June 5, 1957

CIGARETTE SMOKING LINKED TO CANCER IN HIGH DEGREE

American Society Makes Final Report on Study of 187,783 Men—Industry Disputes Statistical Studies

SMOKERS ASSURED IN INDUSTRY STUDY

Report by Tobacco Council Finds No Cigarette Link to Cancer and Heart Disease

The New York Times, August 17, 1964

More often, they've flat-out denied and discredited the scientific consensus.

> No causal link between smoking and disease has been established.
>
> Edward Horrigan Jr., R. J. Reynolds tobacco company, 1982

> The fact is that there is nothing about smoking, or about the nicotine in cigarettes, that would prevent smokers from quitting. Unlike heroin, cocaine or even alcohol, cigarettes do not impair a smoker's ability to think clearly—about smoking or about quitting. If a smoker wants to quit, it may take willpower, but that is all it takes.
>
> Jo Spach, R. J. Reynolds, 1990

The allegation that smoking cigarettes is addictive is part of a growing and disturbing

February 5, 1978. A Herblock Cartoon, © The Herb Block Foundation.

trend that has destroyed the meaning of the term by characterizing virtually any enjoyable activity as addictive, whether it's eating sweets, drinking coffee, playing video games, or watching TV.

> James Johnston,
> R. J. Reynolds CEO, 1994

This was the industry line. At the same hearing at which Johnston spoke, the CEOs of seven major tobacco companies were asked under oath at a congressional hearing whether they truly believed nicotine was not addictive, as their opening statements had implied:

> I believe nicotine is not addictive, yes.
> William Campbell, Philip Morris, 1994

Mr. Congressman, cigarettes and nicotine clearly do not meet the classic definition of addiction. There is no intoxication.

> James Johnston, R. J. Reynolds, 1994

I don't believe that nicotine or our products are addictive.

> Joseph Taddeo, President, U.S. Tobacco
> Company, 1994

I believe that nicotine is not addictive.

> Andrew Tisch,
> Lorillard Tobacco Company, 1994

I believe that nicotine is not addictive.
Edward Horrigan, Liggett Group Inc., 1994

TOBACCO CHIEFS SAY CIGARETTES AREN'T ADDICTIVE

The New York Times, April 15, 1994

> I believe that nicotine is not addictive.
>
> Thomas Sandefur, Brown and
> Williamson Tobacco Corp., 1994

> And I, too, believe that nicotine is not addictive.
>
> Donald Johnston,
> American Tobacco Company, 1994

In fact, a report released six years earlier by U.S. surgeon general C. Everett Koop, drawing on over 2,000 scientific articles and the work of more than 50 scientists, had concluded that nicotine is as addictive as heroin or cocaine. "Its conclusions reflected the growing belief among experts that the use of tobacco should be viewed as a serious form of addiction, rather than simply a dangerous habit," the *New York Times* reported.

Still, some of the politicians bankrolled by the tobacco industry have parroted similar nonsensical denials:

> Office workers are routinely exposed to a variety of so-called carcinogens in the workplace, from sources as varied as spray cleaners and tap water. And yet there is no call . . . to eliminate every trace of these products from the workplace.
>
> Sen. Mitch McConnell of Kentucky, 1993

"THEY KEEP TALKING ABOUT LIFE AND DEATH— WE'VE GOT MONEY AT STAKE HERE!"

January 12, 1979. A Herblock Cartoon, © The Herb Block Foundation.

(In fact, McConnell's statement appears to have been drafted by the Tobacco Institute, an industry group.)

Time for a quick reality check. Despite the hysteria from the political class and the media, smoking doesn't kill.

Then-candidate for U.S. House of Representatives (and future Vice President) Mike Pence, 2001

Even after all the legal and legislative progress toward curbing smoking, each year, nearly half a million Americans die prematurely of smoking or exposure to secondhand smoke, according to the Centers for Disease Control and Prevention. Another 16 million live with a serious illness caused by smoking.

C·A·S·E S·T·U·D·Y

CLIMATE CHANGE

Wake up, America. With all the hysteria, all the fear, all the phony science, could it be that man made global warming is the greatest hoax ever perpetrated on the American people? I believe it is.

Sen. James Inhofe of Oklahoma, 2003

Inhofe was mocked for bringing a snowball into Senate chambers during a Washington, DC, winter storm in 2015 to "prove" so-called global warming wasn't real. This wasn't the first time opponents of taking action on climate change had made such a claim: The

STUDY FINDS WARMING TREND THAT COULD RAISE SEA LEVELS

The New York Times, August 22, 1981

planet isn't warming; or if it is, humans aren't responsible; or if they are, it might not be a bad thing. Ultimately, climate change is where the *It's Not a Problem* mindset might end up doing the most catastrophic damage of all.

It wasn't always this way. Four decades ago, the front page of the *New York Times* trumpeted a study that sounded the alarm on the warming trend. In the years that followed, U.S. and global leaders, Democrats and Republicans, and even some oil and gas titans, committed themselves to action. But as it became clear that major changes to the way the fossil fuel industries did business would be needed, those industries and the politicians that do their bidding began a coordinated PR campaign to muddy up the issue.

Although George H. W. Bush campaigned to become the "environmental president," once in office, the Texas oil and gas man set about negating the consensus on climate change. His chief of staff, John Sununu, called the Senate testimony of leading climate scientist James Hansen "technical garbage" and "poppycock" and warned White House staff to drop the issue:

> *I don't want anyone in this administration without a scientific background using "climate change" or "global warming" ever again. If you don't have a technical basis for policy, don't run around making decisions on the basis of newspaper headlines.*
>
> John Sununu, 1989

> *greenhouse [effect] is still deeply embedded in scientific uncertainty.*
>
> Duane LeVine, Exxon, 1989

That same year, fossil fuel and other companies formed the Global Climate Coalition (GCC), which aimed to thwart action on the issue. "Throughout the 1990s, even as other nations took action," the prominent environmentalist and writer Bill McKibben has written, the GCC "managed to make American journalists treat the accelerating warming as a he-said-she-said story."

In 1992 the GCC distributed a ludicrous documentary, *The Greening of Planet Earth*, which argued that "a doubling of the CO_2 content of the atmosphere" was a good thing and would lead to an expansion of agricultural lands, a flowering of deserts and larger forests. None of the documentary's participants were climate scientists:

GLOBAL WARMING HAS BEGUN, *Expert Tells Senate*

Sharp Cut in Burning of Fossil Fuels Is Urged to Battle Shift in Climate

The New York Times, June 24, 1988

Exxon, whose own research had previously shown that climate change was real and that fossil fuels were a major contributor, similarly changed its tune:

> *In spite of the rush by some participants in the scientific debate to declare that the science has declared the [enhanced] greenhouse effect a certainty . . . I do not believe such is the case. Enhanced*

> *You should see a real greening of the desert.*
>
> Dr. Sherwood Idso,
> physicist and climate change skeptic,
> 1992

In terms of plant growth, it's nothing but beneficial. We would expect a world in which crop plants would produce about 30 to 40 percent more than they are currently producing.

Dr. Hartwell Allen, agricultural scientist and climate change skeptic, 1992

On the eve of the adoption of the 1997 Kyoto Protocol, in which 192 countries agreed to reduce global warming pollution, Mobil took out a *New York Times* ad (estimated cost: $31,000), titled "Reset the Alarm."

Let's face it; The science of climate change is too uncertain to mandate a plan of action that could plunge economies into turmoil.

Mobil, 1997

Although President Bill Clinton signed the treaty in 1998, the Senate refused to ratify it. Industry and its backers continued to rail against Kyoto, largely using arguments crafted by GCC, until President George W. Bush withdrew from the pact in 2001:

Global warming is a myth. The [Kyoto] global warming treaty is a disaster. There, I said it. Just like the "new ice age" scare of the 1970's, the environmental movement has found a new chant for their latest 'chicken little' attempt to raise taxes

and grow centralized governmental power. The chant is "the sky is warming! the sky is warming!"

Mike Pence, 2000

The titans of the fossil fuel industry continue to say even if the earth is warming, it might even be good for you!

The Earth will be able to support enormously more people because a far greater land area will be available to produce food.

Energy magnate and right-wing philanthropist David Koch, 2010

Even as the earth's warming has become harder to dispute, some have continued to cling to denialism. The late radio bully Rush Limbaugh had his own deep thoughts:

I have a theory about global warming and why people think it's real. Go back 30, 40 years when there was much less air conditioning in the country. When you didn't have air conditioning and you left the house, it may in fact have gotten a little cooler out there, because sometimes houses become hot boxes. Especially if you're on the second or third floor of a house in the summertime and all you've got is open windows and maybe a window fan. Or you have some servant standing there fanning you with a piece of paper. When you walked outside, no big deal, it's still hot as hell. Now, 30, 40 years later, all this air conditioning, and it's a huge difference when you go outside. When you go outside now, my golly, is it hot. Oh. Global warming! It's all about the baseline you're using for comparison.

Rush Limbaugh, 2011

And here's President Donald Trump, going full Inhofe:

In the beautiful Midwest, windchill temperatures are reaching minus 60 degrees, the coldest ever recorded. In the coming days, it is expected to get even colder. People can't last outside even for minutes. What the hell is going on with Global Warming? Please come back fast, we need you!

Donald Trump, 2019

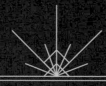

CHAPTER 2

THE FREE MARKET KNOWS BEST

> *We are close to the line where government expansion must stop, or our free enterprise system is lost.*
>
> Sen. Robert Taft of Ohio, 1949

> *Left to their own devices, it is alleged, businessmen would attempt to sell unsafe food and drugs, fraudulent securities, and shoddy buildings. . . . What collectivists refuse to recognize is that it is in the self-interest of every businessman to have a reputation for honest dealings and a quality product. . . . Thus the incentive to scrupulous performance operates on all levels of a given field of production. It is a built-in safeguard of a free enterprise system.*
>
> Alan Greenspan, 1963

DENIAL DOESN'T ALWAYS WORK. SOMETIMES GREEDY corporate leaders and their political lackeys are forced by reality to admit there *might* be some issues with things like workplace conditions, consumer safety or pollution—*perhaps*. In these cases, they often fall back on another time-honored defense: Any problems the free market might have—and it doesn't have many—can be solved by . . . you guessed it . . . the free market itself. This is just another brazen attempt to distort reality while protecting their own power and profits. Unfortunately, sometimes it works.

Of course, the United States has never once relied on an unfettered free market. Economic development, back to the country's earliest days, has always depended on a mix of private investment and targeted government intervention, including publicly run

Cartoon by Steve Sack.

enterprises like the military, schools, the post office, and the network of roads by which farmers bring goods to market. We are, as is commonly and honestly said, "a mixed economy."

During the Great Depression, however, as government expanded to address an urgent national crisis of joblessness and poverty, some opponents of action began to argue that a system of pure "free enterprise" was central—economically, politically and even morally—to the identity of the United States and to the lofty "American Experiment." With the rise of socialism in Europe and a more activist government at home, free enterprise came to stand not merely for a capitalist economic system, but for American democracy and political freedom. The free market, said Ogden Mills, a former Hoover administration treasury secretary and New York senator, was inseparable from "the maintenance of our economic and political system as it developed over a century and a half of amazing progress."

This claim has given free-market arguments their staying power. If any threat to the free market is a threat to Americanism itself, those who want a more fair, inclusive government are un-American. Just as important, the burden of proof always rests on reformers to show beyond doubt that the problem is serious enough, and that no alternative solutions exist, to justify interfering with the market. Those defending the flawed status quo must meet no such burden because the free market is seen as America's natural state of affairs.

Few people dispute that there are times when letting the market work makes sense. If you're still paying for cable TV, you'd be paying a lot less if we allowed for more free-market competition among providers.

But not everything works that way. Sometimes consumers don't have enough information to make smart choices. Sometimes workers lack the bargaining power to demand needed safety measures. Sometimes store owners choose to discriminate, even it costs them Black or gay customers. That's when government needs to step in—not to destroy or replace the free market, but to ensure that it is functioning fairly.

Of course, in the age of chronic inequality, the gig economy, and climate change, it's harder than it used to be to argue that the free market has all the answers. That hasn't stopped those looking to protect their profits from continuing their "leave the free market alone!" histrionics into today . . .

IT IS IMPORTANT TO PUBLIC HEALTH, THEREFORE, THAT *Government regulations* SHOULD NOT HAMSTRING THE MEDICAL ADVANCES PRODUCED BY THE INDUSTRY. —EUGENE M. BEESLEY, 1962

Virtually every New Deal proposal to help workers, homeowners, and the unemployed during the Great Depression drew the ire of corporate titans and their Congressional allies as antithetical to a free-market economy. Pro-reform forces won when they convinced American politicians that these changes were essential to preserving the American experiment. But it didn't happen overnight. Elites fought every element of the New Deal.

From progressive taxation . . .

Income and inheritance taxes, which are in effect confiscatory, destroy themselves by transferring capital in private hands, essential to private enterprise, to unproductive public funds.

Chicago Daily Tribune, 1932

. . . to unemployment benefits:

> *It would result in further and unnecessary intrusion of the Government into the domain of private enterprise, thus aggravating the hardships which have already been caused industry by extensive government regulations, restrictions, and competition.*
>
> James Donnelly, Illinois Manufacturers Association, 1934

The same was true of later efforts to guarantee drug safety:

> *It is important to public health, therefore, that Government regulations should not hamstring the medical advances produced by the industry. Disease and death can result from unnecessary delay in permitting a lifesaving drug to reach the public.*
>
> Eugene M. Beesley,
> Pharmaceutical Manufacturers Association, 1962

And chemical safety:

> *Many companies have cut back drastically their research efforts on new pesticides and diverted their funds to defensive research. . . . Legislation and regulation may ban products but replacements cannot be regulated into existence.*
>
> R. E. Naegele, Dow Chemical, 1971

In the first three decades of the twentieth century, over 68,000 coal miners were killed on the job—more than six per day. Attempts to regulate the mining industry met the same opposition: *We've got this! The free market says so!*

> *In recent years the accident record in the bituminous coal industry has continued to improve. The bituminous coal industry is to be congratulated on its accomplishments to date; given the opportunity, it will make further progress. This is a matter of constant education and not one that requires arbitrary legislation.*
>
> Charles Farrington, National Coal Association, 1947

High Pesticide Levels Seen in U.S. Food

The New York Times, February 19, 1999

> *The coal industry accepts its responsibilities for the safe operation of its mines and where regulation achieves greater safety, we have no quarrel. But, where it does not enhance safety, we believe that Federal regulation is misplaced and counterproductive. It's the overregulation and enforcement of the Act as an end in itself that has caused the coal industry most of its problems.*
>
> Ralph Bailey, Consolidation Coal Co., 1977

Early efforts to pass an Equal Pay Act were deemed unnecessary, not only by business leaders but by some labor leaders, too. The free market, with the help of (male-dominated) unions, was on it!

> *We feel that in a free competitive economy, the task of equal pay to women workers is properly within the province of collective bargaining and not of police action by the government.*
>
> George Meany, American Federation of Labor, 1953

Management, of course, agreed with Meany:

> *The act will tend to cause labor unrest and labor disputes and disrupt collective bargaining agreements. In virtually every industry of any size, [employees] are represented by a collective bargaining agent which has negotiated an agreement with the employer covering rates of pay and conditions of employment.*
>
> Arnold Becker, Continental Can Company, 1963

> *We cannot ignore the variables inherent in our private enterprise system, or give all discretion in resolving them to some single group or agency such as the Department of Labor, if we are to continue as free men and women.*
>
> Fred C. Edwards, Armstrong Cork Company, 1963

WE
FEEL THAT
IN A FREE COMPETITIVE
ECONOMY, THE TASK OF
equal pay to women WORKERS
IS PROPERLY WITHIN THE PROVINCE
OF COLLECTIVE BARGAINING AND
NOT OF POLICE ACTION BY THE
GOVERNMENT.
–GEORGE MEANY, 1953

Just about every piece of progressive regulation has been lambasted as an unconscionable assault on private business. The debate over the Occupational Safety and Health Act (OSHA) of 1970, signed by Republican president Richard Nixon, which aimed to protect workers from health risks and serious injuries or death, reached a pinnacle of free-market apologia.

> *In striving to improve safety and healthful conditions in the workplace it is prudent—and it will be productive—to build upon the foundations of successful experiences of American industry working in*

partnership with State and private agencies. We seriously question whether certain of the measures embodied in the proposed legislation will not encumber rather than enhance progress in occupational safety and health.

John O. Logan, Universal Oil Products Company, 1968

And though they worked with (male) union leaders to fight equal-pay-for-women requirements, when it came to health and safety on the job, now industry groups turned against unions.

Prior to the passage of this legislation, certain special-interest groups (i.e. unions) testifying in support of punitive legislation attempted to describe American business management as irresponsible and unsympathetic to safety on the job. . . . We continue to maintain that standard setting should be carried out by an independent board of experts who are not subject to the pressures of special-interest groups.

Richard B. Berman, Chamber of Commerce, 1972

EMPLOYERS
DO NOT
DELIBERATELY ALLOW
WORK CONDITIONS TO EXIST
WHICH CAUSE INJURY OR ILLNESS.
Safety IS *good business.*
–U.S. CHAMBER OF COMMERCE
NEWSLETTER, 1973

Even after OSHA became law, industry groups didn't stop insisting, despite the evidence, that it was unnecessary: The free market always did and always will prevent safety problems! They denied, of course, that the goal was maximizing profits, not worker safety.

Employers do not deliberately allow work conditions to exist which cause injury or illness. Safety is good business.

U.S. Chamber of Commerce newsletter, 1973

In fact, OSHA has likely saved hundreds of thousands of lives. In 1970, the year it was passed, 38 workers were killed on the job every day. By 2020, that figure had dropped to 14, despite a workforce nearly twice as large.

To fight off needed efforts in the 1970s to make consumer products like lawnmowers, toasters, and toys safer, industry often made the same argument: that it too really cares about safety, so no need for government intervention. At other times it made a very different case, one that's perhaps even more shameless: If our customers don't care, we don't either. Either way, let the free market decide!

This approach assumes that all consumers want the same thing. As others have pointed out, the "consumer interest" is not a monolithic interest which is easily identified. While some consumers may want safe, high quality products, other consumers may wish to sacrifice these qualities for a lower price tag.

Lawrence Kraus, Chamber of Commerce, 1973

Also, consumers want "diversity"—including diversity of product safety and durability standards. *(Really?)*

To the extent that [this legislation] seeks to make varying warranties fit into identical standards, it discourages com-

March 25, 1977. A Herblock Cartoon, © The Herb Block Foundation.

petitive diversity from coming into play, and to that extent fails to serve the interests of either consumers or business.

A. S. Yohalem, Chamber of Commerce, 1970

The American auto industry has been one of the most brazen purveyors of the "free market knows best" line. The truth is that they have resisted government regulation in good times—and taken billions of dollars in government funds over the years to stay alive.

Requiring that automakers add safety devices like the turn signal and the seat belt was unwise, the industry insisted, unless and until the free market decided otherwise.

From a commercial standpoint in a competitive marketplace [safety devices must be optional] until a very high proportion of the customers select the item or unless there are compelling reasons for standard installation.

Frederic G. Donner, General Motors, 1965

April 6, 1966. A Herblock Cartoon, © The Herb Block Foundation.

Henry Ford Sees Economic Hazard in Curb on Autos

Calls on Congress to Avoid "Irrational" Safety Steps—Assails Industry Critics

The New York Times, April 16, 1966

Fuel economy standards, too—implemented in response to the energy crisis of the 1970s—would damage the free market:

> *If we sell too many big cars, we'll have to stop building them. Then we'll have to ram small cars down consumers' throats and use dealer incentives to get rid of them so that we can build big cars again. The public is going to rebel because these hard-to-get big cars will then sell for full list or higher when the small cars are being given away.*
>
> Sid Terry, Chrysler, 1976

Every attempt at government-subsidized healthcare reform, of course, provoked knee-jerk defenses of the free market.

From Medicare . . .

> *[The Medicare bill would] set up a health care program which served little or no necessary social purpose and which would be a direct, unwarranted and completely unfair intrusion in private enterprise.*
>
> Raymond E. King Jr.,
> The National Association of Life Underwriters, 1965

. . . to efforts to guarantee that workers keep some access to health insurance when they lose or leave a job, the 1985 measure we now know as COBRA . . .

> *The problem of lack of health insurance for the unemployed will abate as the economy continues to improve and unemployment is reduced. A continuation of the trend toward a reduction in taxation, regulation,*

and interest rates will help to achieve the dual goal of fuller employment and protection against health care costs.

Jan Peter Ozga, U.S. Chamber of Commerce, 1983

. . . to the Affordable Care Act—in particular, its early proposal for a "public option" to let consumers buy into government programs Medicaid or Medicare in places with insufficient free-market competition:

Forcing free market plans to compete with these government-run programs would create an unlevel playing field and inevitably doom true competition.

Sen. Mitch McConnell, Orrin Hatch, Charles Grassley,
Mike Enzi, and Judd Gregg, 2009

Also, the market was—allegedly—looking out for disabled Americans, so there was no need for the Americans with Disabilities Act:

[THE MEDICARE BILL WOULD] SET UP A HEALTH CARE PROGRAM WHICH SERVED LITTLE OR *no* NECESSARY SOCIAL *purpose.*
–RAYMOND E. KING JR., 1965

Small firms who have hired persons with disabilities have found in most cases that the extra effort makes good economic sense. I have no doubt that, faced with the demands of the marketplace, many other small firms will soon learn the same lesson.

Sally Douglas,
National Federation of Independent Business, 1989

The push to get the United States to join the twentieth century in providing family leave for new parents and those caring for sick loved ones took until 1993, when President Bill Clinton signed the Family and Medical Leave Act (FMLA). Unlike in most other industrialized countries, the law didn't provide paid leave, only unpaid. Still, the FMLA's opponents—including Clinton's predecessor, George H. W. Bush, who vetoed it—voiced the usual complaint: The free market is already taking care of this!

> *We must also recognize that mandated benefits may limit the ability of some employers to provide other benefits of importance to their employees. The number of innovative benefit plans will continue to grow as employers endeavor to attract and keep skilled workers. Mandated benefits raise the risk of stifling the development of such innovative benefit plans.*
>
> George H. W. Bush, 1990

The proposed Employment Non-Discrimination Act (ENDA) had similar problems:

> *ENDA should be opposed by anyone who believes in freedom of speech, freedom of association, and a free market economy.*
>
> Peter Sprigg, Family Research Council, 2013

Efforts to regulate banking and credit card industry practices likewise unnecessarily interfere with free-market competition:

> *The subprime mortgage market, which makes funds available to borrowers with impaired credit or little or no credit history, offers a good example of competition at work.*
>
> Jeffrey Gunther, Cato Institute, 2000

> *If you compare what the card industry looked like 20 years ago to how it looks today, you'll be astonished at how much better a deal consumers are lately getting. And government regulation isn't what drove the improvement; free-market innovation and competition did.*
> Thomas Brown, financial columnist, Bankstocks.com, 2009

Of course, the subprime mortgage market helped tank the economy in 2008 and led to the loss of millions of dollars in household wealth for those who faced foreclosure—and also for their neighbors, who saw their home values plummet in those years. Meanwhile, the 2009 law that cracked down on deceptive "gotcha" credit card fees? It saved consumers over $16 billion in its first five years, suggesting the industry was a long way from effectively regulating itself.

THE *subprime mortgage market,* WHICH MAKES FUNDS AVAILABLE TO BORROWERS WITH IMPAIRED CREDIT OR LITTLE OR NO CREDIT HISTORY, OFFERS A GOOD EXAMPLE OF COMPETITION AT WORK.
–JEFFREY GUNTHER, 2000

The first decades of the twenty-first century haven't been great for the idea that the free market can solve any problem. The 2008 financial crash and the Great Recession that followed; endemic economic inequality; the increasingly precarious position of workers at giant corporations in today's gig economy; the dangerously warming planet—all of these things have made it much tougher to use "But the free market!" as a conversation-ender. Still, some opponents of President Joe Biden's ambitious 2021 "Build Back Better" plan to patch up the frayed social safety net, rebuild our decaying infrastructure, and fight climate change trotted it out just the same . . .

Most of the programs in the plan are redistribution of wealth programs that undermine job-creating free-market activity.

Brian Darling,
lobbyist and former aide to Senator Rand Paul, 2021

The Biden model is so heavily taxing and regulating private enterprise that it will not pay after tax to work, invest or take risks. You know, safety nets are one thing, but it's free enterprise that drives the American economic machine. . . . Mr. Biden doesn't believe in free enterprise.

Larry Kudlow, former top economic adviser to President
Trump, 2021

Quite simply, the plan is a rejection of the American system of free enterprise and basic economics.

Heritage Foundation report, 2021

C·A·S·E S·T·U·D·Y

CIVIL RIGHTS: "A STEP TOWARD THE DESTRUCTION OF FREE ENTERPRISE"

There may be no more perverse example of free market fetishism than its application to the defense of racist Jim Crow laws in the South, as well as racially discriminatory practices in the North.

Sure, plenty of people openly admitted their racism. Others preferred instead to defend the principle of "free enterprise," which let them make their case to a new set of potential allies. If some white business owners wanted to serve Black people, they argued, that's OK. But if they don't, it's anti-American to force them. Doing so could destroy our system of free enterprise!

These arguments against anti-racism measures got particularly loud as the federal government debated expanding, and making permanent, the 1941 Fair Employment Practices Committee, which banned discrimination in World War II-related work:

> *Another nail in the coffin of free enterprise.*
> **Sen. Albert W. Hawkes of New Jersey, 1945**

> *[The FEPC is] a step toward the destruction of free enterprise.*
> **Southern employers, 1948**

The opposition to fair hiring succeeded for a time. Not until 1964 did Congress establish the Equal Employment Opportunities Commission.

When one southern senator announced the formation of the Federation for Constitutional Government, a precursor to white supremacist citizens' councils, he framed the issue as one of market freedoms:

> *Our organization will carry on its banner the slogan of free enterprise.*
> **Sen. James Eastland of Mississippi, 1955**

And when sit-ins and boycotts began in the late 1940s and continuing into the 1960s, they, too, were a threat to free enterprise:

> *[Free enterprise] includes not only freedom from undue government interference but also freedom to select its own methods of doing business free from picketing, boycotting, or other coercive tactics of a coercive minority.*
>
> Conservative attorney
> Frank F. Nesbit, 1947

> *This lunch counter was his property. Did he not have a right to control its use?*
>
> James J. Kilpatrick,
> conservative writer, 1962

Those cries grew louder when President Lyndon B. Johnson proposed the 1964 Civil Rights Act:

> *I am having nothing to do with enforcing a law that will destroy our free enterprise system.*
> Gov. George Wallace of Alabama, 1964

> *[The bill authorizes] such vast governmental control over free enterprise in this country as to commence the process of socialism.*
>
> Sen. Richard Russell of Georgia, 1964

Segregation supporters used "free enterprise" to defend their right to discriminate, mainly against Black Americans, which hardly seems a good example of freedom—except maybe for white people:

> *We have a divine right to discriminate. . . . Every person who is engaged in business has a right to choose the customers of his business.*
>
> Restaurant owner Lester Maddox,
> future governor of Georgia, 1963

After the Civil Rights Act passed, ending segregation in most places and making discrimination on the basis of race, gender, or religion illegal, Maddox led a march for "freedom"—and segregation—promoting "states' rights, property rights and free enterprise." When the U.S. Supreme Court upheld the Civil Rights Act, Maddox said that it portended "the death of the American free enterprise system" and closed his restaurant. He reopened it as a museum: "a shrine to the free enterprise system."

Outside the South, these arguments met with agreement from free-enterprise fetishists—who were often at pains to make clear they themselves weren't racist:

> *Private racism is not a legal, but a moral issue— and can be fought only by private means, such as*

economic boycott or social ostracism. Needless to say, if that "civil rights" bill is passed, it will be the worst breach of property rights in the sorry record of American history in respect to that subject.

Free-market evangelist
and author Ayn Rand, 1963

Is there any difference in principle between the taste that leads a householder to prefer an attractive servant to an ugly one and the taste that leads another to prefer a Negro to a white or a white to a Negro, except that we sympathize and agree with the one taste and may not agree with the other? I deplore what seems to me the prejudice and narrowness of outlook of those whose tastes differ from mine in this respect and I think less of them for it. But in a society based on free discussion, the appropriate recourse is for me to seek to persuade them that their tastes are bad and that they should change their views and their behavior, not to use coercive power to enforce my tastes and my attitudes on others.

Libertarian economist Milton Friedman, 1962

Friedman wasn't just any economist, of course. He was perhaps the most influential economic thinker of his generation, and his work on monetary policy, regulation, and other topics—which, by and large, advocated for a reduced government role in the economy—undergirded much of U.S. economic policy during the 1980s and for decades after. Friedman reduced racism to a question of "taste," blind to the reality that endemic racism might not be eradicable by market forces alone—a blindness shared by many of his disciples. That helps account for the many ways in which the economy continues to fail Black and brown people, from persistent racial disparities in employment and wages to chronic underfunding of federal efforts to root out on-the-job discrimination.

Even though the Civil Rights Act of 1964 and the Voting Rights Act of 1965 became mostly settled law in the next decades, there remained free enterprise absolutists who believed legislating racial equality violates that sacred system:

The start of the evil can be pinpointed precisely: the monstrous Civil Rights Act of 1964. . . . If I am an employer and, for whatever reason, I wish to hire only five-foot-four albinos, I should have the absolute right to do so. Period.

Libertarian economist Murray Rothbard, 1991

One popular 12-term Texas congressman agreed:

The Civil Rights Act of 1964 gave the federal government unprecedented power over the hiring, employee relations, and customer service practices of every business in the country. The result was a massive violation of the rights of private property and contract, which are the bedrocks of free society. The federal government has no legitimate authority to infringe on the rights of private property owners to use their property as they please and to form (or not form) contracts with terms mutually agreeable to all parties.

Rep. Ron Paul of Texas, 2004

And the congressman begat a son:

A free society will abide unofficial, private discrimination—even when that means allowing hate-filled groups to exclude people based on the color of their skin.

Rand Paul, 2002

During his successful 2010 campaign for the U.S. Senate, Rand Paul was forced, uncomfortably, to elaborate on his view that the Civil Rights Act, while perhaps in some ways necessary, should not have prohibited private businesses from discriminating:

I think it's a bad business decision to exclude anybody from your restaurant—but, at the same time, I do believe in private ownership. I absolutely think there should be no discrimination in anything that gets any public funding, and that's most of what I think the Civil Rights Act was about in my mind.

Rand Paul, 2010

Asked if it would be acceptable for Rev. Martin Luther King Jr. not to be served at the counter at Woolworth's, Paul added:

I would not go to that Woolworth's, and I would stand up in my community and say that it is abhorrent, um, but, the hard part—and this is the hard part about believing in freedom . . . In a free society, we will tolerate boorish people, who have abhorrent behavior, but if we're civilized people, we publicly criticize that, and don't belong to those groups, or don't associate with those people.

Rand Paul, 2010

Paul's opinion can still be found not only in the hallowed halls of the Senate but in the heights of academia, too:

Libertarians should not only oppose Title II [of the Civil Rights Act, which barred racial discrimination in public accommodations]; they should shout that opposition from the highest roof tops. . . . By violating the principle that private property is private, Title II created a precedent for other policies that violate property rights and have far less justification than Title II.

One example is smoking bans in restaurants. . . . Similar considerations apply to occupational health and safety regulation. Once workplaces are somehow "public," the door is open for the state to pursue various goals that libertarians find objectionable. Mandatory maternity leave is a good example.

Jeffrey Miron, Harvard economist and Cato Institute scholar, 2010

In other words, if we start shutting down racist businesses, pretty soon we'll have to protect workers on the job and give new mothers time with their babies. The horror.

FACEBOOK'S "BIG TOBACCO MOMENT"

In late 2021, the parallels became impossible to ignore: Social media giants, especially Facebook, knew a great deal about the toxic impact of their products, particularly on children, while denying any problem exists—much as the tobacco industry had for decades. "Facebook and Big Tech," one senator declared, "are facing a Big Tobacco moment."

That senator, by the way, was Richard Blumenthal of Connecticut, who led a successful suit against Big Tobacco as his state's attorney general in the 1990s. The comparison is of course inexact: Children did not develop asthma from inhaling Instagram fumes, and users aren't dying of Facebook-related cancers. Children did suffer, though, sometimes profoundly, from the way the social media giant delivered its products to them. Like Camel cigarettes did with the old "Joe Camel" ads, Facebook has pioneered efforts to reach an ever-younger audience, especially with its popular photo-sharing platform Instagram.

Company-commissioned research showed the harm it could do. "We make body image issues worse for one in three teen girls," internal Facebook research on Instagram use among teen girls concluded in 2019. "Teens blame Instagram for increases in the rate of anxiety and depression. This reaction was unprompted and consistent across all groups."

Company leaders have at times responded with denial:

> The research that we've seen is that using social apps to connect with other people can have positive mental-health benefits.
>
> Mark Zuckerberg,
> 2021

After congressional testimony by former employee and whistleblower Frances Haugen, who copied tens of thousands of internal documents before she left the company in 2021, the company came back with the standard free-market justification—if there's a problem, it's in our interest to fix it!

In the months after Haugen's testimony, Facebook lost its aura of invulnerability. Once regarded as a uniquely brilliant business that could do no wrong, Facebook was suddenly revealed to be just as clueless and morally suspect as any other big corporation that profits from the insecurities of children.

On February 3, 2022, Facebook set an ignominious record as its stock dipped by $232 billion, marking the largest single-day drop in value for any company in Wall Street history. And in October of 2022, Facebook's parent company Meta fell out of the top 20 most valuable companies in the world, inspiring Zuckerberg to announce tens of thousands of layoffs in what he termed a "year of efficiency" for the company. Facebook still has hundreds of billions of dollars to burn, but consumers are approaching their products with newly skeptical eyes.

> I don't know any tech company that sets out to build products that make people angry or depressed. The moral, business, and product incentives all point in the opposite direction.
> Mark Zuckerberg, 2021

CHAPTER 3

IT'S NOT OUR FAULT,
IT'S YOUR FAULT

> *Legislation cannot remedy the evils which result from the perversity of human nature.*
>
> coal industry trade bulletin, 1910
>
> *[Do] we really want to subsidize the losers' mortgages?*
>
> CNBC anchor Rick Santelli, 2009

THERE'S ANOTHER COMEBACK THAT SHAMELESS, PROFIT-maximizing corporations and their brown-nosing political and media backers like to use when problems become too large to ignore, and potential threats to their money and power loom on the horizon:

OK, maybe it is a problem. But it's not our fault! In fact, it's your fault!

Time and again, we hear that sick workers or injured consumers have no one to blame but themselves. The obvious solution, it follows, shouldn't be to require companies to adopt safety measures but rather to convince regular people to change their behavior—to *be more careful!* For industry, blaming the victim comes with an obvious additional benefit: It renders the victim less sympathetic, making the public less supportive of taking action to fix the problem.

Yes, all those warning labels on products are there for a reason. Individual people make plenty of dumb decisions all the time. However, corporations spend millions on design and marketing and have access to much more information about the potential dangers their products pose to workers, consumers, or the public. As such, they are chiefly responsible when things go wrong. If their factories or products are safe only for people who make smart decisions 100 percent of the time, or who are healthy already, or who are able to avoid addiction or dependence, then they're not safe at all.

The notion that it's unfair to use government regulation to fix a problem if individual people can be shown to have made mistakes gets things backward. By making it harder for drug companies to sell addictive prescription medication, or for banks to push home loans to unqualified buyers, we protect people from making many of these mistakes in the first place. That's the whole point. Government should protect consumers, as well as corporations who do right by their customers (sometimes sacrificing maximizing profits in the process), while discouraging corrupt profiteers.

Or maybe we're looking too closely at this one. For those who use this line, the point is to deflect blame so that they keep profiting from doing what they're doing. No matter who gets hurt.

EITHER SOMETHING WENT WRONG FROM A NATURAL/UNNATURAL MANNER THAT WAS NOT FORESEEABLE BY US OR HUMAN BEINGS, OR *somebody made a mistake* OR SOMETHING.
—DON BLANKENSHIP, 2010

In the coal mining industry, a long history of devastating accidents and wanton disregard for worker safety spawned novel ways of blaming coal miners themselves. These arguments, unbelievably, have continued for over a century.

After a coal mine collapsed in West Virginia in 1903, killing an undetermined number of miners, the state blamed dead and injured workers for irresponsibly standing under an unsafe roof.

> *Such accidents are little short of deliberate suicide. No legislation can reach such cases as this.*
>
> James Paul,
> West Virginia's chief mine inspector, 1903

For many decades, the mining industry echoed those arguments.

> *[The bill will] not strike at the fundamental cause of accidents, which in the main is the carelessness on the part of men, cured only by education.*
>
> Charles Farrington, National Coal Association, 1946

> *Training and education in themselves are no panacea for the industry's accident problem. What, in addition, must be done is to find a way to motivate people to think and work safely. All miners must want to observe safety laws, rules, and regulations, and perform their daily task without endangering themselves and their fellow workers.*
>
> Ralph Bailey,
> Consolidation Coal Company, 1977

After a 2010 disaster at Massey Energy's Upper Big Branch Mine in Montcoal, West Virginia, killed 29 miners, the company's CEO suggested his dead employees might have been at fault:

> *Either something went wrong from a natural/unnatural manner that was not foreseeable by us or human beings, or somebody made a mistake or something.*
>
> Don Blankenship, Massey Energy, 2010

Blankenship served a year in prison after his 2015 conviction on a misdemeanor charge of conspiring to willfully violate mine safety and health standards—a conviction he called "a badge of honor" in West Virginia.

The coal industry wasn't the only one to try to dodge regulation by blaming workers for safety issues. The decades-long effort to eliminate lead from products ranging from dyes to paint to gasoline found manufacturers frequently arguing that the problem was not their fault, but that of "careless" employees:

> *The only tendency toward illness comes to men who are intemperate in their habits. In every case of poisoning I have heard of, the man was an exceedingly hard drinker. . . . Where the men are temperate in their habits I never found a case.*
>
> Arthur S. Summers, a manufacturer of "dry colors" that contained lead, 1912

> *The essential thing necessary to safely handle [tetraethyl lead] was careful discipline of our men. . . . It becomes dangerous due to carelessness of the men in handling it.*
>
> Thomas Midgley Jr., General Motors, 1925

Or sometimes it was the parents' fault:

> *The only seemingly feasible means of coping with the childhood plumbism [lead poisoning] problem is that of parental education.*
>
> Lead Industry Association bulletin, 1950

I HAVE YET TO SEE A WOMAN IN A MANUFACTURING ESTABLISHMENT WHO HAS BEEN ABLE TO RISE TO THE TOP IN A MANUFACTURING JOB . . . IT IS BECAUSE MEN IN GENERAL, I THINK, LIKE TO BE SUPERVISED BY *men* RATHER THAN *women* IN FACTORY JOBS.
—WILLIAM MILLER, 1963

Even pay inequities between men and women can be blamed on women if you try hard enough. Women don't land management roles because men just don't want to work for them, which is women's fault:

> *I have yet to see a woman in a manufacturing establishment who has been able to rise to the top in a manufacturing job. . . . It is because men in general, I think, like to be supervised by men rather than women in factory jobs.*
>
> William Miller, U.S. Chamber of Commerce, 1963

Or maybe women fabricate a problem where none exists:

> *You can't really blame the U.S. Chamber of Commerce, for instance, for opposing the bill, chivalrous at heart as its members may be. For in addition to the possibility of added costs, there's this problem: It's a rare woman, we gather, who doesn't think she is discriminated against on payday.*
>
> *Wall Street Journal* editorial, 1962

Auto safety laws, too, are of minimal value—the real problem is reckless drivers, or as they were often called, "the nut behind the wheel." When Congress first mulled auto safety standards in the 1960s, in response to a growing number of deaths and injuries on the road, industry was desperate to pass the buck.

> *Roads, laws and cars are inanimate of themselves. They cannot give— or take—life. It is people who animate highway transportation; people who use the roads—obey or do not obey the laws—drive carefully or carelessly.*
>
> H. E. Humphreys Jr.,
> Chairman of the United States Rubber Co., 1964

In the same year that Mr. Humphreys made that remark, the United States Rubber Company's sales hit a record high of $237 million in the first quarter, a 20 percent increase in earnings from 1963.

A few years later, lawmakers debated the measure that would become OSHA—that's the one that's likely saved hundreds of thousands of lives by protecting workers on the job, you'll remember. Industry voices and their political allies warned that it would do little to curb injuries because they were the result, as one charged, of "unsafe acts," not "unsafe conditions."

PEOPLE WHO DON'T STAND OUT IN *the sun*—IT DOESN'T AFFECT THEM.
–U.S. SECRETARY OF THE INTERIOR DONALD HODEL, 1987

> *The really important progress in occupational safety and health would require far more consideration of the man rather than the environment.*
>
> Leo Teplow, American Iron and Steel Institute, 1968

> *We find that 80 to 90 percent of the injuries which are occurring in our company are due to a human failure rather than a piece of equipment, a machine, or so on.*
>
> J. Sharp Queener, Du Pont Co., 1968

> *The vast majority of accidents result from human failings. No amount of legislation against employers is going to stop an employee who decides to take a shortcut in his job or to shed his steel-toed shoes or safety helmet.*
>
> *Nation's Business,*
> the U.S. Chamber of Commerce magazine, 1968

[We don't] believe safety can be achieved through legislation, but only through education. Automotive regulatory laws are a good example. If a law states that a specific speed may not be exceeded without a penalty, does it stop speeding?

William Naumann,
Associated General Contractors of America, 1968

Um, at the risk of stating the obvious: Yes, speeding laws do indeed help stop speeding. When the 55-mile-an-hour speed limit was repealed, there was an almost 10 percent increase in road fatalities on rural interstates and a 4 percent increase on urban ones.

When a movement arose to restrict or eliminate cotton dust in mill work—because it led to a dangerous, if not fatal, condition called "brown lung"—again the workers often took the blame:

The [cotton dust] problem is grossly exaggerated. There are subjective symptoms which the patients express that sometimes result from bronchitis, emphysema, or excessive smoking.

F. Sadler Love,
American Textile Manufacturers Institute, 1977

When scientists and environmental activists began pushing to eliminate chlorofluorocarbons, a compound in many aerosol products that damaged the ozone layer, one novel defense held that it was only a problem for those who got too much sun:

People who don't stand out in the sun—it doesn't affect them.
U.S. Secretary of the Interior Donald Hodel, 1987

As limits on alcohol advertising came to be proposed in the 1990s, the industry argued that legislation was unnecessary; again, the issue was personal responsibility:

> *Every individual chooses if and how he or she will use our products. In a free society, we can only encourage wise choices, legislating them has never worked.*
>
> Anheuser-Busch full-page ad in
> *New York Times* and *USA Today*, 1991

Same with the movement to reduce unhealthy foods and promote labeling on menus and food packaging to let consumers know what they're eating:

> *I wouldn't say we're part of the [obesity] problem. There are not good or bad foods. There are good and bad diets. This does come down to personal responsibility.*
>
> Steven Anderson,
> National Restaurant Association, 2003

> *Our position is that the individual who is concerned about obesity should emphasize healthy lifestyle, personal responsibility, regular exercise, and moderation. Seventy-six percent of all meals are prepared at home. That's where nutrition has to start.*
>
> Dale Florio, legislative counsel for
> the New Jersey Restaurant Association, 2005

Of course, it's hard for people to take responsibility when you're actively fighting to deny them the information they'd need to make responsible choices. . . .

_____

The tobacco industry has fought regulation with an array of specious arguments, but one of their favorites is to blame smokers for getting addicted to cigarettes:

> *The decision to smoke or not to smoke is a personal decision. Anyone who has not heard or read the surgeon general's warnings would have had to be a cave dweller. . . . You can't legislate personal behavior.*
>
> Tobacco Institute, 1978

> *When you've got on the label for 20 years that cigarettes can kill you, how can you sue?*
>
> John C. Maxwell, tobacco analyst, 1985

When Purdue Pharma introduced its opioid painkiller OxyContin in 1996, the company went into overdrive to make sure its new product dominated the prescription market. It did, but soon the drug came under scrutiny for a sharp rise in both addiction and overdoses. States, cities, and counties sued, charging that the company's aggressive pursuit of business and misleading information about the drug's addictiveness, were responsible for the nation's opioid epidemic.

Purdue execs struck back. In internal emails later released as part of a lawsuit, they plotted a strategy of claiming those addicted to the drug, not the drug itself, were the real problem.

KEY MESSAGES THAT WORK . . . IT'S NOT *addiction,* IT'S *abuse.* —PURDUE PHARMA STRATEGY MEMO, 2008

> *We have to hammer on the abusers in every way possible. They are the culprits and the problem. They are reckless criminals.*
>
> Purdue Pharma CEO Richard Sackler, 2001

> *We intend to stay the course and speak out for people in pain—who far outnumber the drug addicts abusing our product.*
>
> Richard Sackler, 2001

> *KEY MESSAGES THAT WORK . . . It's not addiction, it's abuse.*
>
> Purdue Pharma strategy memo, 2008

In fact, as court documents would show, the company knew exactly what was causing the opioid epidemic. An internal note from then-Purdue CEO Craig Landau in 2017 described the problem this way: "There are: Too many Rxs being written/Too high a dose/For too long/For conditions that often don't require them/By doctors who lack the requisite training in how to use them appropriately."

In September 2019, facing 2,900 lawsuits, Purdue filed for bankruptcy restructuring. Two years later, a federal settlement dissolved the company. The Sackler family, which controlled Purdue, agreed to pay $4.5 billion that will mainly go to addiction treatment and prevention programs.

Former Head of OxyContin Maker Purdue Pharma Denies Blame for Opioid Crisis

CBS News, August 18, 2021

Many plaintiffs attacked the judgment as inadequate and objected to provisions that effectively absolved the Sacklers of personal liability: They never had to admit it was *their* fault.

———

When the economy almost collapsed in 2008, it was thanks largely to risky lending practices by profiteering banks and investment companies. Wall Street and its defenders saw a different culprit: homeowners—disproportionately lower-income and non-white—who, lured by lending companies, had taken on mortgages they couldn't afford. And they wanted to make sure those unfortunate borrowers didn't get any government help.

One financial journalist became instantly famous for a rant, delivered on the floor of the Chicago Mercantile Exchange, about these "losers." It was credited with launching the anti-government Tea Party movement:

THERE'S ONE GIANT PATERNAL *elephant in the room* THAT HAS SLIPPED NOTICE: HOW ILLEGAL IMMIGRATION, CRIME-ENABLING BANKS, AND OPEN-BORDERS BUSH POLICIES FUELED THE *mortgage crisis.*
—MICHELLE MALKIN, 2008

> *The government is promoting bad behavior. . . . How about this, President and new administration? Why don't you put up a website to have people vote on the internet as a referendum to see if we really want to subsidize the losers' mortgages; or would we like to at least buy cars and buy houses in foreclosure and give them to people that might have a chance to actually prosper down the road, and reward people that could carry the water instead of drink the water?*
>
> *How many of you people want to pay for your neighbor's mortgage that has an extra bathroom and can't pay their bills? Raise their hand.*
>
> Rick Santelli, CNBC, 2009

Santelli wasn't alone in scapegoating borrowers who were lured or duped by aggressive bank marketing to take on loans that were too big for them to handle.

> *It wasn't the Bush administration as much as it was Democrats in Congress who were pushing the lending institutions to get out there and lend more money, even to unqualified buyers—to the minorities, to the poor, to the young—so that everyone could own a home.*
>
> Sen. Jon Kyl of Arizona, 2008

Conservative gadfly Michelle Malkin found a way to blame the crash on all of the above—but also on illegal immigration.

> *The Mother of All Bailouts has many fathers. As panicked politicians prepare to fork over $1 trillion in taxpayer funding to rescue the financial industry, they've fingered regulation, deregulation, Fannie Mae and Freddie Mac, the Community Reinvestment Act, Jimmy Carter, Bill Clinton, both Bushes, greedy banks, greedy borrowers, greedy short-sellers, and minority homeownership mau-mauers (can't call 'em greedy, that would be racist) for blame.*
>
> *But there's one giant paternal elephant in the room that has slipped notice: how illegal immigration, crime-enabling banks, and open-borders Bush policies fueled the mortgage crisis.*
>
> Michelle Malkin, 2008

Americans own almost 415 million guns, nearly half of the world's total number of civilian-held firearms. Researchers say they are at least part of the reason the country has more violence than other developed nations. Most American gun owners support common-sense gun safety laws, but the extreme wing of the gun lobby, represented by the National Rifle Association and other groups bankrolled by profit-hungry gun manufacturers, has controlled the debate and blocked promising reforms.

They insist that "responsible" gun owners don't need government direction—and blame the "irresponsible" for any problems, which they insist are beyond the reach of law. In other words: It's *their* fault.

> *There are two wildly different gun cultures in our country. One is the freedom-loving, gun-rights culture that upholds the responsible use of guns for hunting, sport and self-defense. The other is the criminal culture that thrives in the places where government restricts gun rights.*
>
> Frank Miniter, editor-in-chief of
> the NRA magazine *America's 1st Freedom*, 2018

For extremists, the problem is never guns, but the supposedly mentally ill people who abuse them.

> *We don't go around shooting people, the sick people do. They need to be fixed.*
>
> A gun owner protesting a Connecticut gun safety measure after the Sandy Hook Elementary School massacre killed 26 people, 2013

WE HAVE NO NATIONAL DATABASE OF THESE *lunatics* . . . WE HAVE A COMPLETELY CRACKED MENTALLY ILL SYSTEM THAT'S GOT THESE *monsters* WALKING THE STREETS. —WAYNE LAPIERRE, AFTER SANDY HOOK MASSACRE, 2012

> *We have no national database of these lunatics . . . We have a completely cracked mentally ill system that's got these monsters walking the streets.*
>
> NRA president Wayne LaPierre, after Sandy Hook, 2012

In fact, research shows that having access to a gun is a bigger risk factor for violence than being diagnosed with mental illness. Despite his stated concern about mental health, LaPierre nevertheless opposes putting more criminal and mental health records into the federal background check system, saying the system is really about "one thing—registering your guns."

TORT REFORM

The blaming-the-victim strategy hasn't just been a way for corporations to fight off needed regulation. They've also used it to go on offense.

In the 1980s, insurance companies and big corporations began pushing "tort reform"—a campaign aimed at making it harder to use the courts to hold corporations accountable when people were harmed by faulty products. Jury awards against corporate defendants were out of control, went the argument. Part of the problem, according to the business lobby, was that people wanted to blame companies for things that were really their own fault.

In 1992, 79-year-old Stella Liebeck became Exhibit A in the case for tort reform when she sued McDonald's after spilling hot coffee on her lap while sitting in the passenger seat of a parked car.

It sounded absurd: The woman did it to herself, business and its allies pointed out. How was McDonald's to blame? ABC News has called the case "the poster child for excessive lawsuits."

In fact, McDonald's had a policy of serving their coffee at between 180 and 190 degrees—hotter than any of their competitors. As a result, the burns that Liebeck sustained on her thighs, genitals, and buttocks were so severe that she was hospitalized for a week and needed skin grafts. She sued only after asking McDonald's to cover her medical bills, when they topped $10,000; the burger giant offered her $800.

For those pushing tort reform, however, those details didn't fit the story:

> *A lady goes to a fast-food restaurant, puts coffee in her lap, burns her legs, and sues and gets a big settlement. That in and of itself is enough to tell you why we need tort reform.*
> Rep. John Kasich of Ohio, ranking member of the House Budget Committee, 1994

The real problem, according to a leading tort reform lobby group, was that no one takes personal responsibility anymore:

> *Every action we take in life carries with it some risk. The question is, when do we take*

personal responsibility for our actions—and their consequences—and when is it OK to blame others? CALA advocates an end to the "blame game," the increasing practice by many in society to use lawsuits to solve a problem rather than taking personal responsibility for the consequences of their actions.

Citizens Against Legal Abuse (CALA) website

McDonald's defense lawyers took a similar tack: blaming and mocking Liebeck and other victims. When Liebeck's lawyers wanted to introduce testimony from two other women who had been scalded by the burger chain's brew, defense lawyers objected:

First-person accounts by sundry women whose nether regions have been scorched by McDonald's coffee might well be worthy of Oprah. But they have no place in a court of law.

Tracy McGee, lawyer for McDonald's, 1994

McDonald's also suggested Liebeck was partly to blame because she held the cup between her legs—she was trying to add cream and sugar, and said the car had no flat surfaces—and didn't immediately remove her clothes:

If the plaintiff was injured and damaged as alleged, then her injuries and damages were the result of her own negligence or of the negligence of a third person or party for whom this Defendant may not be held responsible.

McDonald's lawyers, 1994

Also, McDonald's suggested, it was Liebeck's fault for being so old, because skin gets thinner and more vulnerable as people age:

Mrs. Liebeck's age may have caused her injuries to have been worse than they might have been in a younger individual.

McDonald's lawyers, 1994

A New Mexico jury heard all the facts and awarded Liebeck $2.9 million. That was later reduced by a judge to $640,000—but the case quickly took on a life of its own in the media as an example of America's culture of litigiousness. Jay Leno made Liebeck into the butt of his late-night jokes. Talk radio went wild. It was referenced on *Seinfeld*, and, years later, in a popular country song:

Plasma gettin' bigger, Jesus gettin' smaller,

> *Spill a cup of coffee, make a million dollars.*
> Toby Keith, "American Ride," 2009

Just about everyone agreed Liebeck was at fault for her carelessness:

> *Anyone who's ever bought take-out beverages knows lids leak. You're about as likely to find a leak-less beverage lid as you are to discover a brand of pantyhose that never runs. Spill avoidance depends on the juggling ability of motorists who eat, drink and drive all at once.*
> *Philadelphia Daily News* editorial, 1995

One writer saw a trend, grouping Liebeck with two other people who sued after spilling hot restaurant food or drinks on themselves—though neither of the other two won a penny:

> *What do Stella Liebeck, Alecia Wallace and Bryce R. McNaughton have in common? It never occurred to any of them that holding a cup of something very hot directly over their laps is not a good idea.*
>
> Zay Smith, *Chicago Sun-Times* columnist, 1995

The result was to cement a perception in the minds of even casual news consumers that frivolous lawsuits were out of control, and reform was urgently needed.

Soon, the floodgates opened. Newt Gingrich and congressional Republicans quickly added a tort reform plank to their Contract with America platform for the 1994 midterms. The next year, Texas passed seven different major bills that made it harder for people to win damages against big businesses, hospitals, and insurers. Over the following decade, numerous other states passed similar packages, and the issue was a major theme of Texas governor George W. Bush's successful run for president in 2000.

Stella Liebeck died in 2004, still upset about how she was portrayed in the case. "I was not in it for the money," she said years later. "I was in it because I wanted them to bring the temperature down, so that other people would not go through what I did."

CHAPTER 4

IT'S A JOB KILLER

> *Never in the history of the world has any measure been brought in here so insidiously designed so as to prevent business recovery, to enslave workers, and to prevent any possibility of the employers providing work for the people.*
>
> Rep. John Taber of New York, 1935, opposing Social Security

FROM THE DAWN OF WORKPLACE SAFETY STANDARDS IN the Progressive Era, through the New Deal, through Clinton- and Obama-era reforms, up to the battles over COVID-19 relief, most attempts to economically support struggling Americans had one big problem, according to greedy industry leaders and industry-funded politicians: They would kill jobs. Maybe even whole industries. Possibly the entire economy. Businesses have used this ludicrous line in almost the exact same form—sometimes verbatim—for more than a century. Over and over and over again.

The Job Killer lie is effective in part because it's versatile. As we'll see, you can use it to fight almost any kind of policy advance that might possibly shave a few pennies off corporate profits, from raising taxes on big corporations, to family leave, to health, safety, and

environmental protections, to the minimum wage. After all, it's almost always *possible* that some businesses might respond to potential new costs by cutting hiring or laying off workers—and it's hard for reformers to disprove that possibility in advance.

Of course, plenty of other things could happen, too. Some businesses innovate to reduce the cost of new regulations. Others find that new laws increasing worker pay or requiring leave end up reducing turnover and boosting employee morale and performance enough to cancel out the costs. Generally, studies show that increasing worker pay doesn't result in cost hikes or job losses, because when more workers have more money, they spend that money in local businesses. Likewise, paid family leave and sick day laws reduce turnover, boost employee morale, and increase job performance, which all boost the bottom line.

That's why history shows that the cries of Job Killer rarely pan out. In fact, the almost three-decade-long economic boom following World War II was a period when corporations and the wealthy paid a far higher tax rate, when profits were shared far more equally, and when worker protections were stronger than today. More recently, there's little evidence that the states and cities that have raised their minimum wage to $15 an hour lately have seen big job losses in response, despite industry's warnings of impending disaster.

Not that this is ultimately about reality. The Job Killer myth, like other corporate lies, is mainly designed to instill fear and anxiety, a natural human reaction to the idea of change. Which is why, despite being disproved so often in the past, it's still with us today.

[FIRE CODE RULES WILL LEAD TO] THE *wiping out* OF INDUSTRY IN THIS STATE.
—SPOKESMAN FOR NEW YORK MANUFACTURERS, 1913

The 1911 Triangle Shirtwaist Factory Fire in New York City killed 146 workers, most of them immigrant women and girls, largely because exit doors were locked and other safety precautions were ignored. The disaster led to a dramatic series of reform proposals, including fire code and other safety standards. But local business leaders warned the rules would destroy them.

> *[Fire code rules will lead to] the wiping out of industry in this state.*
> Spokesman for New York manufacturers, 1913

> *The Real Estate Board of New York is informed that thousands of factories are migrating to New Jersey and Connecticut in order to be freed from the oppressive laws of New York State.*
> George W. Olvany, Real Estate Board of New York, 1914

That wasn't true. A state commission didn't find a single case of a manufacturer leaving the state because of the new laws, the *New York Times* reported in 1914.

The New Deal provoked the same objections. Social Security has transformed American life dramatically for the better, lifting more people out of poverty each year than any other government program. Polls consistently show overwhelming public support for the program and strong opposition to cutting benefits.

But from the earliest debates, it was denounced as a job killer.

> *[The Social Security bill would] discourage employment rather than encourage it.*
>
> James Emery, National Association of Manufacturers, 1935

> *Do not forget this: Such an excessive tax on payrolls is beyond question a tax on employment. In prosperous times it slows down the advance of wages and holds back re-employment. In bad times it increases unemployment, and unemployment breaks wage scales.*
>
> Alf Landon, Republican nominee for president, 1936

Corporations and their allies likewise trashed unemployment benefits, contained in the same package of Depression-era New Deal reforms as a means of providing a lifeline to those out of work:

> *Employers pay men, not machines. Can there be any question but that this and similar legislation will drive industry faster and faster toward mechanization? Can there be any question but that its normal tendency will be to depress wages, since the higher the total payroll, the greater the taxes? Can there be any question but that it will retard reemployment of men and intensify the development of machinery and its substitution for men?*
>
> John C. Gall, National Association of Manufacturers, 1934

> *It will hasten mechanization of all processes and thus permanently reduce employment. It will force employers to keep wage rates at the lowest possible minimum and thus reduce the amount of the tax.*
>
> George Lucas, Publishers Association, 1934

Some argued that the Equal Pay Act of 1963 might help women, but it would cost men jobs:

> *We have had several young men start out as secretaries and later rise to positions of importance. . . . When these young men started, and as they progressed, I am certain that their wages were higher than some female secretaries doing equal or superior work. But we also knew that there was a possible potential of their rising to more important jobs, supervising a large number of men. If this law is passed, we will hire women for all secretarial positions and be deprived of this avenue of advancement.*
>
> William Miller, U.S. Chamber of Commerce, 1963

Oh, and it would cost women jobs, too:

> *I know that there are variables from plant to plant and business to business, and that if an attempt is made to regiment all industrial relations, individual businesses will suffer—their employees, especially women, can face unemployment—and the national economy will be weakened.*
>
> Fred C. Edwards, Armstrong Cork Company, 1963

> *[Consider] the possible impact of this bill upon efforts to equalize wages in plants employing mostly women and relatively few men. If there is a wage differential between men and women that cannot be justified under the restrictive standards of this bill and the wages of the male employees cannot be reduced, a plant could run*

UNDER THE GUISE OF *civil rights* FOR THE DISABLED, THE SENATE HAD PASSED A *disaster* FOR U.S. BUSINESS. —NATIONAL REVIEW, 1990

> *into serious financial difficulty if it were forced to increase the pay of all female employees to the level of the few male members.*
>
> John B. Olverson, Electronic Industries Association, 1963

It's not just women who must accept being discriminated against. Equal access for disabled Americans via the Americans with Disabilities Act? Also not something the nation could afford.

> *Under the guise of civil rights for the disabled, the Senate had passed a disaster for U.S. business.*
>
> *National Review,* 1990

Of course, every attempt at environmental and chemical regulation has provoked the same charge, from Progressive Era and New Deal reforms, through the passage of the Clean Air and Water Acts, up to efforts to combat climate change.

Drug safety standards proposed in the New Deal reform package might save lives, industry warned, but they'd also kill jobs:

> *[The bill] will seriously affect employment and morale in the industries indicated. It will put thousands of men and women out of work. It will close dozens of manufacturing plants and hundreds of stores. . . . It will hurt thousands. . . . It will help none.*
>
> New York Board of Trade, 1938

Early attempts to reduce water pollution met the same objection:

We would strenuously object to any bill that would make it unlawful to allow water from the anthracite mines or breakers to enter the streams adjacent. . . . The anthracite industry would be put out of business overnight if such laws were passed and enforced.

Henry H. Otto, Hudson Coal Co., 1947

Later efforts to ban ozone-depleting chemicals, too, could be disastrous:

Entire industries could fold.

Joseph P. Glas, Du Pont Corp., 1988

The Clean Air Act Amendments of 1990? Guaranteed to cost jobs, according to business:

The effects include serious long-term losses in domestic output and employment, heavy cost burdens on manufacturing industries, and a resultant gradual contraction of the entire industrial base. The irony of this bleak scenario is that these economic hardships are borne with no real assurance they would be balanced by a cleaner, healthier environment.

National Association of Manufacturers, 1987

[IT WOULD NOT BE POSSIBLE] TO ACHIEVE THE *control* LEVELS SPECIFIED IN THE BILL . . . MANUFACTURERS . . . WOULD BE FORCED TO *shut down.*
—AMERICAN AUTOMOBILE MANUFACTURERS ASSOCIATION, 1970

This study leaves little doubt that a minimum of 200,000 (plus) jobs will be quickly lost, with plants closing in dozens of states. This number could easily exceed 1 million jobs—and even 2 million jobs—at the more extreme assumptions about residual risk.

The Business Roundtable, lobbyist association, 1990

In fact, a 2011 study by the U.S. Environmental Protection Agency found that, thanks to increased health and productivity among workers, as well as savings on medical expenses, the law's economic benefits amounted to $2 trillion, over 30 times its costs of $65 billion.

The auto industry has been a particularly valiant promoter of the job-killer line when faced with efforts to combat pollution. The Clean Air Act of 1970, for instance, could destroy more than just the auto industry:

> *This bill could prevent continued production of automobiles . . . [and] is a threat to the entire American economy and to every person in America.*
>
> Lee Iacocca, Ford Motor Company, 1970

> *[It would not be possible] to achieve the control levels specified in the bill . . . manufacturers . . . would be forced to shut down.*
>
> American Automobile Manufacturers Association, 1970

We saw in an earlier chapter how automakers denounced laws aimed at increasing fuel efficiency, known as Corporate Average Fuel Economy (CAFE) standards, as intrusions on the sacred working of the free market. But in case that didn't work, they also called them job killers:

> *With the Environmental Protection Agency laws, we'd either have to shut down or break the law, and we aren't going to break the law.*
>
> Henry Ford II, 1976

> *The whole CAFE scheme is, in terms of public policy, ridiculous, and has the practical effects of driving U.S. jobs abroad.*
>
> Former Transportation Secretary Jim Burnley, 1989

Same for the Family and Medical Leave Act (FMLA): It not only offended the principle of free enterprise, as we've seen, but also would destroy jobs and perhaps entire businesses:

> *[Family leave laws are] the greatest threats to small business in America.*
>
> John Sloane Jr.,
> National Federation of Independent Businesses, 1987

> *It is a job killer. . . . It makes it more expensive to hire people, so businesses say we won't hire people. . . . You would be telling businesses, through that act, that they are required to bring temporaries in, go through a training cycle, and lose the continuity that is so important to making a business function well. It has the effect of making it more expensive for them to do business. More expensive per employee, more expensive per job. The business can only defend itself by offering fewer jobs.*
>
> Rep. Ernest Istook of Oklahoma, 1992

> *The real world impact of this well-intentioned legislation—this mandate—is that employers will revisit those projections and budgets and cut back on something else, including creating new jobs at the very time that we need new jobs.*
>
> Sen. Bob Dole of Kansas, 1992

> *[The Democratic Party doesn't] get that the ability of American businesses to create jobs is directly related to the burden government places on their backs. They don't get that mandating family and medical leave is just one more burden added. . . . Mandating that business pick up the tab for these benefits allows them to advance their agendas without spending federal dollars.*
>
> Rep. Tom DeLay of Texas, 1993

> *There is nothing pro-family about putting people out of work—but that is exactly what this bill does. Estimates are that tens of thousands of working men and women will be put out of work if this bill passes.*
>
> Rep. Rodney Grams of Minnesota, 1993

These dire predictions appear not to have been borne out. A 2000 U.S. Department of Labor survey of affected businesses found that over 90 percent said the law had had either no noticeable effect or a positive effect on profitability.

Nevertheless, state legislation to create paid family leave programs—the federal law provides only unpaid leave—has been fought with the same arguments:

> *[California] can follow the programs of Germany and France and get unemployment way up into double digits. That's the result of bad legislation.*
>
> Mark Sappenfield,
> *The Christian Science Monitor, 2004*

> *I hope this is a lesson for the next Republican governor or next Republican president before they sign this kind of bill. Once Democrats control everything they are going to start raising taxes and raising benefits to pay for these screwball ideas. . . . A tax on a job eliminates jobs; this is a tax on a job.*
>
> State Sen. Ray Haynes of California, 2002

In fact, California employers surveyed in 2011 reported that the program had had either a positive effect or no noticeable effect on productivity, profitability and performance, turnover, and morale.

What really kills jobs, corporations and the rich have long insisted, are tax hikes. In fact, the line goes, they're a surefire way to tank the entire economy. Perhaps never was that argument made more vociferously than in the effort to kill President Bill Clinton's 1993 budget bill, which increased corporate taxes, individual taxes for the wealthy, and the capital gains tax rate:

> *These new taxes will stifle economic growth, destroy jobs, reduce revenues, and increase the deficit. Economists across the ideological spectrum are convinced that the Clinton tax increases will lead to widespread job loss.*
>
> Rep. Phil Crane of Illinois, 1993

> *Clearly, this is a job killer in the short-run. . . . The impact on job creation is going to be devastating, and the American young people*

> *in particular will suffer a fairly substantial deferment of their lives because there simply won't be jobs for the next two to three years to go around to our young graduates across the country.*
>
> Rep. Dick Armey of Texas, 1993

> *We're going to find out whether we have higher deficits, we're going to find out whether we have a slower economy, we're going to find out what's going to happen to interest rates, and it's our bet that this is a job killer.*
>
> Rep. John Kasich of Ohio, 1993

[WE HAVE] HIGH UNEMPLOYMENT BECAUSE SMALL BUSINESSES, PEOPLE WHO MAKE *$250,000 a year,* ARE NOT SPENDING AND INVESTING AND IT WILL GET WORSE IF WE DON'T EXTEND THOSE *tax cuts.*
—SEAN HANNITY, 2010

None of that happened. At least 22 million jobs were created during Clinton's tenure, a bigger percentage gain than under any other president since the economic boom of the 1960s. For good measure, by 2000, the budget deficit had been erased and there was a surplus of $236 billion.

And yet, when President Barack Obama unveiled a plan to raise taxes on the wealthy nearly two decades later, opponents trotted out the same lines:

> *The Obama Tax Plan Would Eliminate Hundreds of Thousands of Jobs Each Year. . . . In other words, for Americans who are unemployed now, their prospects of employment would worsen under the Obama tax plan.*
>
> Heritage Foundation study, 2010

[We have] high unemployment because small businesses, people who make $250,000 a year, are not spending and investing and it will get worse if we don't extend those tax cuts.

Fox News anchor Sean Hannity, 2010

In fact, the economy netted 11.6 million jobs over Obama's two terms in office, a gain of 8.6 percent, despite Obama taking office during the country's worst financial crisis since the Great Depression. A 2016 study by a respected University of California, Berkeley, economist found that the Obama tax hikes did not hurt the economy or slow economic growth.

C·A·S·E S·T·U·D·Y

THE MINIMUM WAGE: A MAXIMUM JOB KILLER?

There may be no progressive reform more frequently reviled as a job killer than the minimum wage. Going back to the Fair Labor Standards Act of 1938—which established a federal minimum wage, created a right to overtime pay, and restricted child labor, among other advances—employers have repeatedly insisted it would only hurt the people it was meant to help, by killing jobs:

> *High hourly wages mean nothing to a worker if he has no job.*
>
> C. C. Shephard,
> Southern States Industrial Council, 1938

> *What profiteth the laborer of the South if he gain the enactment of a wage and hour law—40 cents per hour and 40 hours per week—if he then lose the opportunity to work?*
>
> Rep. John McClellan of Arkansas, 1938

Those same arguments continued into the 1960s and beyond:

> *An increase of $0.25 per hour in the minimum wage would raise the unemployment rate for non-white teenagers by 8 percent.*
>
> Arthur Burns, economist and future chair of the Federal Reserve, 1966

GOVERNOR VETOES $1.50 MINIMUM PAY

New Bill Is Likely   *New York Times, April 17, 1965*

If the minimum wage were increased to anywhere between the low of $2.50 and the high of $3.00, between 2 and 3.1 million jobs would be lost.

Robert T. Thompson,
U.S. Chamber of Commerce, 1975

I am vitally concerned about the thousands of teenagers and young adults who will either lose their jobs or be rendered unemployable in the unskilled labor markets as the result of increasing the minimum wage to $2.50 or more per hour.

Rep. Eldon Rudd of Arizona, 1977

The consequences of minimum wage laws have been almost wholly bad, to increase unemployment and to increase poverty.

Milton Friedman, 1970s (exact date unknown)

The minimum wage has caused more misery and unemployment than anything since the Great Depression.

Ronald Reagan, 1980

By the late Reagan years, these claims about the minimum wage were so broadly accepted—including by many economists—that the nation's leading news-paper could publish an editorial titled "The Right Minimum Wage: $0.00."

April 3, 1996. A Herblock Cartoon, © The Herb Block Foundation.

> *Those at greatest risk from a higher minimum would be young, poor workers who already face formidable barriers to getting and keeping jobs.*
>
> New York Times, 1987

> *Work is what low-income people really need, and what they deserve from our society. We ought not force them off the work rolls and on the welfare rolls as a result of raising the minimum wage.*
>
> Rep. Robert Walker of Pennsylvania, 1989

> *Now, what is the effect of this law? Indeed, I admit, some will have a mandated pay raise in America. Those will be the lucky ones. Many more will have their hours cut. . . . Many will lose their jobs. And again, thousands, thousands will be denied that opportunity to climb on that first rung of the economic ladder in America and, instead, be condemned to a life of poverty. This should not happen in America.*
>
> Rep. Jeb Hensarling of Texas, 2010

As of early 2022, the federal minimum wage was last raised in July 2009, to $7.25 an hour. This is the longest workers have gone without a minimum wage increase since it was created. The wage is now worth 21 percent less than it was in 2009, and 34 percent less than in 1968, according to the Economic Policy Institute.

> *Look, I wish we could just pass a law saying everybody should make more money without any adverse consequences. The problem is you're costing jobs from those who are just trying to get entry level jobs.*
>
> Rep. Paul Ryan of Wisconsin, 2013

> *In fact, the impact of minimum wage usually is that businesses hire less people. . . . We have a lot of history to prove that raising the minimum wage does not grow the middle class.*
>
> Sen. Marco Rubio of Florida, 2013

Have these predictions of doom been borne out? The irony is that even as politicians and pundits stubbornly clung to the "job killer" rhetoric, a revolution in empirical economics was reshaping the academic consensus. In 1993, when economists David Card and Alan Krueger analyzed a natural experiment comparing a minimum wage hike in New Jersey to neighboring Pennsylvania, finding "no indication that the rise in the minimum wage reduced employment," one Nobel Prize-winning economist

High New Jersey Minimum Wage Doesn't Seem to Deter Fast-Food Hiring, Study Finds

The New York Times, May 20, 1993

was so scandalized by the heresy that he penned a *Wall Street Journal* editorial decrying the authors as "camp-following whores." But since then, numerous economists have replicated their efforts and found similar results.

More recently, economists Paul K. Sonn and Yannet M. Lathrop from the National Employment Law Project, a labor-backed group, analyzed data from all 22 increases in the federal minimum wage since 1938. They found that employment actually increased one year after a wage hike 68 percent of the time. Perhaps the most comprehensive recent analysis was conducted by the University of Massachusetts Amherst economist Arindrajit Dube and three colleagues. They looked at 138 state-level minimum-wage increases between 1979 and 2016 and found that in the five years after the wage went up, the number of low-wage jobs "remained essentially unchanged."

Armed with real data, the academic consensus has so entirely flipped over the past 30 years that Card was awarded the 2021 Nobel Prize in Economics for his groundbreaking minimum wage research.

SEATTLE'S MINIMUM WAGE

While the federal government wouldn't help hourly workers, a growing number of states and localities have. In 2014, a coalition of labor and community leaders pushed the city of Seattle to raise the minimum wage from $9.47 per hour to $15 per hour over several years. Some Seattle business groups and their allies spoke out against the wage hike, predicting—predictably—that it would kill jobs:

> You'll see businesses moving or not forming here, and making decisions to hire fewer workers or have fewer hours for those workers.
>
> Peter Nickerson, Seattle economic consultant, 2014

> They're [small businesses] the most likely to fail. Their daily income will be less than their labor costs. This is a significant increase in a very short period of time, and they will not be able to change their business models in order to meet this new law.
>
> Craig Dawson, CEO of Seattle payments-processing company, 2014

The restaurant industry, critics of the law claimed, was uniquely vulnerable to the wage hike:

> Every [restaurant] operator I'm talking to is in panic mode, trying to figure out what the new world will look like.
>
> Washington Restaurant Association CEO Anthony Anton, 2015

> As the implementation date for Seattle's strict $15 per hour minimum wage law approaches, the city is experiencing a rising trend in restaurant closures. . . . The shutdowns have idled dozens of low-wage workers, the very people advocates say the wage law is supposed to help. Instead of deliver-

ing the promised "living wage" of $15 an hour, economic realities created by the new law have dropped the hourly wage for these workers to zero.

Washington Policy Center, 2015

What actually happened?

A rigorous 2017 study of Seattle's food-service industry by researchers at the University of California, Berkeley, found that wages increased after implementation while employment remained unaffected. The same researchers in 2018 studied the food-service industry in six cities (including Seattle) that had raised the wage to $15, and found basically the same story: Raising the wage led to increased earnings and no clear decrease in employment. "Our models estimate employment effects of a 10 percent increase in the minimum wage that range from a 0.3 percent decrease to a 1.1 percent increase, on average," the researchers wrote. Meanwhile, a University of Washington researcher who went into his study a minimum wage skeptic was ulti-

mately moved to write a mea culpa after finding similar results: "Despite the fact that the work of our UW research team has been held up as supporting an anti-minimum wage agenda, I come away from this work more inclined to support reasonable minimum wage increases."

But Seattle restaurateurs and diners didn't need economists to tell them that the local restaurant scene was booming. By 2017, the number of restaurants licensed in Seattle was up 25 percent from a decade earlier, creating a labor shortage that pushed wages up well above minimum. U.S. Bureau of Labor Statistics data bears this out. A 10-year chart of local restaurant employment shows a steady upward sloping line with no evidence of an impact from the minimum wage hikes that occurred in the middle. For years after Seattle passed its $15 minimum wage, King County was consistently one of the top large counties in both wage and employment growth, according to the bureau's Quarterly Census of Employment and Wages program.

CHAPTER 5

YOU'LL ONLY MAKE
IT WORSE

The federal government declared war on poverty, and poverty won.

President Ronald Reagan, 1988

"They're Simple, Happy Folk — Knowledge Would Just Confuse Them"

April 19, 1967. A Herblock Cartoon, © The Herb Block Foundation

PLUTOCRATS AND POLITICIANS INVESTED IN THE STATUS quo understand that they won't win hearts and minds if they come across as selfish or lacking compassion. So, when fighting efforts to end slavery, enfranchise women, raise wages, or reduce poverty, one favorite tactic is to piously insist that their real concern isn't for their own profits or power. Nothing could be further from their minds!

What they're really worried about, you see, is that well-intended reforms will backfire, leaving the people they're supposed to help even worse off than before, often by sapping their will to work and lulling them into dependence on government—a government they've spent decades depicting as incompetent, so that's obviously a terrible outcome. In short, you're harming the very people you're trying to help! That's how you get the frankly absurd spectacle of business groups like the U.S. Chamber of Commerce or the National Association of Manufacturers warning with deep concern that pro-worker policies will in fact hurt workers.

Given that the stated and open mission of these groups is to advocate for corporate interests, not those of their employees, it's a little hard to take their concerns at face value. Because we know: their goal is to increase profits—workers' economic security and the broader public interest be damned.

Whether this pose of concern is believable might not much matter. For those invested in the status quo, it's yet another way to distract from the obvious reality: It's their own interests they're worried about, not anyone else's.

———————

THE
IDLE WILL *beg* IN
PREFERENCE TO WORKING;
RELIEF IS EXTENDED TO THEM
WITHOUT SUITABLE DISCRIMINATION.
THEY ARE NOT LEFT TO FEEL THE *just*
consequences OF THEIR IDLENESS.
—ADMINISTRATORS OF POOR RELIEF,
BEVERLY, MASSACHUSETTS,
MID-1800S

Nowhere has the claim that reform hurts those it is meant to help been more damaging than in the 200-year wrangle over programs for poor Americans—as well as formerly secure Americans suddenly down on their luck due to a recession, a health crisis, or in our era, the COVID-19 pandemic. When Reagan made his false claim that poverty programs didn't help those in poverty, he gave a generation of voters suffering compassion fatigue—and perhaps a touch of racism?—permission to oppose efforts to help the poor. Because those efforts were actually hurting them!

Such claims have a much longer history. Going back to the nineteenth-century days of "outdoor relief"—forms of assistance like cash, food, heating supplies, and clothing, provided at home—as well as grim poorhouses, there have always been those who argue that boosting struggling Americans only rewards indolence and degrades their morality and will to work:

> *More than 20,000 persons were degraded to the condition of public paupers, deprived of their feelings of honourable independence and self-respect, and ... were exposed to a powerful temptation to practice deception and fraud, had their fears of the consequences of idleness, improvidence and vice at least greatly lessened.*
>
> George Arnold, minister-at-large to the poor in
> New York City, mid-1800s

> *The idle will beg in preference to working; relief is extended to them without suitable discrimination. They are not left to feel the just consequences of their idleness.*
>
> Administrators of poor relief,
> Beverly, Massachusetts, mid-1800s

Unemployment benefits have been accused of promoting laziness and killing off "individualism" ever since the federal law establishing them was proposed during the Great Depression in 1934:

> *[Unemployment Insurance] would increase unemployment by aggravating the very conditions which it is attempting to correct, by crippling the agencies which furnish opportunities for employment, by*

> *discouraging efforts to relieve unemployment, and by placing a premium on idleness.*
>
> James L. Donnelly,
> Illinois Manufacturers Association, 1934

Nearly 80 years later, opponents of jobless benefits were still making that same argument:

> *Now I don't want to sound unnecessarily coldhearted. I like to think I'm compassionate. But supply-side economics is about incentives. And if we re-incentivize unemployment, it will surely diminish the will and the effort of our working people to find new work. That is an economic principle.*
>
> Larry Kudlow, future top Trump economic adviser, 2013

Of course, if jobless benefits sap the will to work, you'd think that establishing or raising the minimum wage would have the opposite effect, increasing workers' motivation by ensuring that they earn enough to live on. Way better than being on the dole! But one remarkably consistent argument by the powerful is to insist that the poor must be motivated only by sticks, while the rich get carrots. So raising the minimum wage is never seen as an incentive to work. In fact, in the view of business interests, it hurts those it seeks to help, by making workers more expensive and so driving employers to reduce hiring:

> *But where will employers obtain the money to pay for that increase? It is unrealistic to assume that somehow the increase will be squeezed out of profits. . . . In plain fact, the burden of an increased minimum*

wage will fall heavily on those least able to bear it. The fringe employers, the unskilled worker, the young and the handicapped are those who will be priced out of the job market.

Anthony J. Obadal, Labor Relations Manager,
Chamber of Commerce, 1970

Under these inflationary pressures many of the industries and small businesses employing marginally trained or unskilled workers will be forced to cut back on the number of those employees or go out of business. The very worker that the federal minimum wage was intended to aid will find himself out of work.

Rep. Mickey Edwards of Oklahoma, 1977

It might even be racist, they say:

I've often said that the minimum-wage rate is the most anti-Negro law on the books.

Milton Friedman, 1973

MINIMUM WAGE LAWS MAY VERY WELL BE THE MOST *anti-poor laws* ENVISIONED BY MODERN GOVERNMENT POLICYMAKERS. —MICHAEL LAFAIVE, 1997

When we pass minimum wage legislation it says one thing, Mr. Speaker: It says to the young black in the inner city, it says to the handicapped individual, it says to the young person looking for a first-time job, unless you can meet a minimum standard, we will pass a law that says it is a violation of the federal statute to hire such a person. . . . Minimum wage laws create unemployment. That is a mean, vicious thing to do.

Rep. Bob McEwen of Ohio, 1989

> *This is an unemployment act that hurts minority youth, and that is a shame.*
>
> Rep. John Shadegg of Arizona, 1996

> *I understand it is called a minimum wage bill but in fact it is a layoff bill. . . . Kids will lose their jobs, minorities will lose their jobs, senior citizens will lose their jobs.*
>
> Rep. Mark Souder of Indiana, 1996

> *Minimum wage laws may very well be the most anti-poor laws envisioned by modern government policymakers.*
>
> Michael LaFaive, Mackinac Center for Public Policy, 1997

Indeed, these days, as a vibrant, labor-backed campaign has inspired a growing number of states and cities to adopt a $15-an-hour minimum, the response from business interests has been the same: You're only hurting yourself!

> *$15 minimum wage hurts workers who need help the most.*
>
> *Bloomberg Opinion* headline, 2019

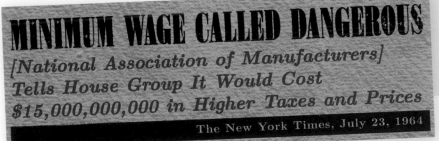

MINIMUM WAGE CALLED DANGEROUS

[National Association of Manufacturers] Tells House Group It Would Cost $15,000,000,000 in Higher Taxes and Prices

The New York Times, July 23, 1964

The same goes for expanding overtime pay:

> *The problem with this left-wing economic engineering is that it might . . . help some people, but it's probably going to hurt a lot of other people. Why should an employer, for instance, increase the hours of its current employees, give a lot of overtime, if it will cost them a lot more? . . . It's going to end up hurting the average worker and laborer.*
>
> Daniel Halper, *Weekly Standard* editor, 2015

And Medicare:

> *[Medicare] could destroy private initiative for our aged to protect themselves with insurance against the cost of illness.*
>
> Sen. Milward Simpson of Wyoming, 1965

Even taxing corporations and the rich just hurts workers, the story goes. President Bill Clinton's 1993 budget was ultimately credited with helping to produce a long economic boom, but that's not how opponents saw it at the time:

> *The impact on job creation is going to be devastating, and the American young people in particular will suffer a fairly substantial deferment of their lives because there simply won't be jobs for the next two to three years to go around to our young graduates across the country.*
>
> Rep. Dick Armey of Texas, 1993

We saw just these types of arguments in 2020, when the COVID-19 pandemic rocked the economy, and policymakers discussed how best to assist the unemployed as well as struggling businesses. Maybe because so many businesses were in the same boat as their employees, at least two large COVID relief packages passed with bipartisan support, which included extended unemployment benefits. But small-government ideologues quickly warned that continuing the aid would discourage work:

> AS RONALD REAGAN ONCE SAID, THE BEST SOCIAL PROGRAM IS A *job*.
> —GOV. KEVIN STITT OF OKLAHOMA, 2021

For decades, the Left has been pushing to keep more Americans trapped in the cycle of government dependency through expansive government programs, ensuring it is more lucrative to stay home than to work. This increases government dependency, catching people in the welfare trap. Unfortunately, recent changes to the unemployment system in response to COVID-19 have presented a new opportunity for the Left to trap Americans at home.

Alli Flick, Foundation for Government Accountability, 2021

U.S. Chamber of Commerce Wants End to $300-A-Week Federal Unemployment Benefits— Blames It On Bad Jobs Report

FORBES, MAY 7, 2021

Many states listened. By late August of 2021, 26 had taken steps to end some or all of the jobless benefits. One was Oklahoma:

> *As Ronald Reagan once said, the best social program is a job.*
> Gov. Kevin Stitt of Oklahoma, 2021

Unemployment Benefits Forever?
Treasury Suggests How States Can Continue the Incentives Not to Work

WALL STREET JOURNAL, AUGUST 20, 2021

One corporate-friendly governor even found a new faux-compassionate angle to justify the move: He was just trying to ease the burden for those who *are* currently employed, by incentivizing others to return to their jobs:

> *It's not fair to the people that are currently in the workforce. They are getting killed right now, they're having to work so many hours. They need some help.*
> Gov. Brian Kemp of Georgia, 2021

And if the goal was to spur hiring, cutting off benefits failed. Job growth was no higher—and perhaps even a bit lower—in states that cut benefits than in states that didn't, U.S. Labor Department numbers showed. A separate study by well-regarded economists looked at 19 states that ended

Cut off of Jobless Benefits Is Found to Get Few Back to Work

Prematurely Ending Federal Programs Had Little Effect on Employment but Sharply Cut Spending, Potentially Hurting State Economies, Researchers Say

THE NEW YORK TIMES, AUGUST 20, 2021

the benefits, and found that workers lost an average of $278 a week in benefits, while gaining just $14 a week in new earnings—largely because only around 13 percent actually found a new job. This loss of income didn't just affect the workers themselves, the study found. It led them to cut their own spending by about 20 percent, hurting their local economies.

It's not just unemployment benefits. Census Bureau figures show that, thanks to the range of pandemic relief from Washington—stimulus payments, child care support, food assistance, and more—the poverty rate fell by 8.5 million in 2020, the largest ever single-year drop. Another study found that child poverty plummeted from 14.2 percent to 5.6 percent—a bigger decline than in the previous 50 years combined.

C·A·S·E S·T·U·D·Y

THE WELFARE DEBATE

> *By taxing the good people to pay for these programs, we are putting a premium on illegitimacy never before known in the world.*
>
> Gov. Orval Faubus of Arkansas, mid-1950s

There's probably no set of public programs more often blamed for hurting their intended beneficiaries than what came to be known as "welfare" for families. It began as a relatively uncontroversial New Deal program, commonly known as a "widow's benefit," to keep children and mothers together in the event of a father's death. Welfare rolls began to rise in the 1950s, however, and many of the mothers were unmarried or divorced, not widowed.

In time, that led to the claim by welfare opponents that generous benefits were behind the growth in out-of-wedlock births, since they allowed single mothers to have kids knowing the government would take care of them. That notion became a common talking point among welfare opponents for decades:

> *Welfare also plays a powerful role in promoting illegitimacy. Research . . . shows, for example, that a 50 percent increase in monthly AFDC and food stamp benefit levels will cause a 43 percent increase in the number of illegitimate births within a state.*
>
> The Heritage Foundation, 1996

President Vetoes Child Care Plan as Irresponsible

He Terms Bill Unworkable and Voices Fear It Would Weaken Role of Family

The New York Times, December 10, 1971

A larger argument gained currency, too: welfare programs were increasing, not decreasing, poverty:

> *Policies that increase dependency, break up families, and destroy self-respect are not progressive; they're reactionary.*
>
> **President Ronald Reagan, 1985**

That idea helped inspire the 1996 welfare reform bill, which slashed direct cash aid to poor families while expanding child care subsidies, Medicaid, and tax credits for those who went to work but remained poor—as many did. The sometimes-liberal *New Republic*, urging President Bill Clinton to sign the bill, depicted the intended target of welfare reform with a cover photo of a Black woman holding a baby and smoking a cigarette, in case anyone missed the point.

Did the law work as intended? One authoritative 2018 Stanford University research overview concluded that "while welfare reform assisted families with incomes close to the poverty threshold, it did less to help families in deep or extreme poverty. Under the current welfare regime, many single mothers are struggling to support their families without income or cash benefits. Even women who are willing to work often cannot find good-paying, steady employment." As for the hope that cutting welfare would lead to more kids growing up in two-parent households, that appears not to have panned out. In 1997, the year after the bill was signed, 68 percent of American kids lived with married parents. In 2017, it was 65 percent.

Not that any of this has changed the minds of those determined to believe that welfare hurts the poor. Paul Ryan, the future House Speaker and 2012 Republican vice presidential nominee, famously divided the American people into "makers and takers," as he sought to cut welfare programs.

> *We don't want to turn the safety net into a hammock that lulls able-bodied people to lives of dependency and complacency, that drains them of their will and their incentive to make the most of their lives.*
>
> **Paul Ryan, 2012**

> *Concern for the poor is often equated with expanding government programs. . . . The reality is that, in many cases, government policy can make it more difficult for those striving to make ends meet.*
>
> **Heritage Foundation report, *Big Government Policies That Hurt the Poor, and How to Address Them*, 2017**

Of course, essentially the opposite is true. One 2012 study found that "access to food stamps in childhood leads to a significant reduction in the incidence of . . . obesity, high blood pressure, and diabetes . . . and, for women, an increase in economic self-sufficiency."

Still, the beat goes on . . .

Getting people off of welfare into a productive job is not just a way to reduce costs, it's a proven way to rebuild broken lives and move people into the mainstream. There is dignity in work. There is despair in welfare. After three generations of the failed entitlement state, hasn't welfare done enough harm to the very people it was supposed to help?

Stephen Moore, co-founder of Club for Growth, Trump economic adviser, 2016

—OH, THOSE UNINTENDED CONSEQUENCES—

When they're not hurting people they're purporting to help, social reformers often get blamed for programs that allegedly result in unintended, even apocalyptic, consequences.

Slavery, for instance:

> We cannot get rid of slavery without producing a greater injury to both the masters and slaves.
>
> Thomas Dew,
> professor and slavery advocate, 1832

And women's suffrage:

> Women's participation in political life . . . would involve the domestic calamity of a deserted home and the loss of the womanly qualities for which refined men adore women and marry them. . . . Doctors tell us, too, that thousands of children would be harmed or killed before birth by the injuri-

ous effect of untimely political excitement on their mothers.

> Henry T. Finck, writer and critic, 1901

Along the same lines, income taxes don't spread wealth, but instead poverty:

> Confiscation of private wealth does not make the public or even its agent, the government, rich. It does not create equality of wealth, but an equality of poverty.
>
> *Chicago Daily Tribune*, 1932

Also, environmental regulation can actually make the environment worse. Take recycling:

> Recycling itself can cause environmental harm. . . . As a result, the environmental costs of recycling may exceed any possible environmental benefits.
>
> Lynn Scarlett, Reason Foundation and the National Center for Policy Analysis, 1991

Along similar lines: Anti-pollution efforts can increase the number of oil spills. By establishing unlimited liability for shipowners, industry warned, a proposed 1990 law that gave the federal government more authority to prevent and respond to catastrophic oil spills could make it impossible for established shipowners to get insurance, leaving the field to irresponsible players more likely to see spills:

> The net result could well be a greater probability of oil spills, less likelihood of a responsible owner to deal with those spills, less reliable transportation of oil and greater cost to the consumer; the very things the U.S. wanted to avoid.
>
> Vernon C. Miller Jr.,
> Skaarup Shipping Corp, 1990

Oh, and auto pollution laws could increase auto pollution:

> The more efficient new cars won't save a drop of gas until they're purchased. If they don't sell, not only energy conservation, but pollution and safety improvements will be set back.
>
> General Motors spokesman, 1975

February 28, 1979. A Herblock Cartoon, © The Herb Block Foundation.

And climate change legislation could worsen climate problems:

If our manufacturers leave, whether for North Carolina or China, and they take their greenhouse gases with them, we might not have solved the problem but exacerbated it instead.

Allan Zaremberg, California Chamber of Commerce president, 2006

If you're sticking your head in the sand, and saying that fossil [fuel] has to be eliminated in America . . . and thinking that's going to clean up the global climate, it won't clean it up at all. If anything, it would be worse.

Sen. Joe Manchin of West Virginia, 2021

CHAPTER 6

IT'S SOCIALISM!

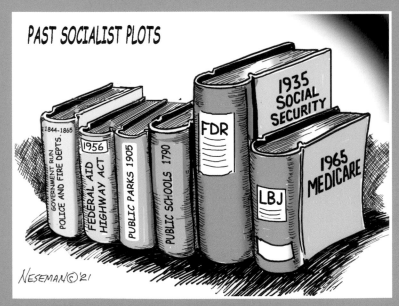

Cartoon by Dale Neseman

EVER SINCE MARX AND ENGELS PUBLISHED *THE Communist Manifesto* in 1848, and socialist movements began to flourish in Europe, the shameless forces of wealth and power have decried all major attempts to create a fairer American society—from taxation to labor standards to civil rights to family leave to government-subsidized healthcare—as socialist, communist, "communistic," "Red," or "Bolshevik." Or—a related fear-mongering tactic—they've warned about the threat to freedom, conjuring the specter of a totalitarian government trampling on cherished liberties. Even more modest initiatives like federally subsidized student loans, wide-scale recycling, and compensating coal miners for black lung have been given the socialist label.

The idea, of course, is that socialism is unpopular in America, so calling an idea "socialist" is a way to discredit it. For many older Americans, the word still evokes the Soviet Union, which for decades we were told was an "evil empire" that oppressed its own citizens and had the capacity to annihilate us at any moment. (To be fair, it might not have had the power to annihilate us, but it did oppress its own citizens—as non-socialist Russia still does, too.) Small wonder that "Socialist!" works as an attack line. Plus, like invocations of the free market, it's a way to paint your opponents as un-American.

It's also glaringly dishonest. Holding powerful interests to reasonable standards and using collective action to solve broad societal problems isn't socialism. On the contrary, these approaches to building prosperity and social stability are the hallmark of successful societies and integral to the American democratic tradition. There can be no true liberty without them. But yes, they do hinder rapacious businesses' ability to exploit workers, consumers, or the environment in the pursuit of profit and power. Nothing antagonizes those at the top more than that.

Still, with several members of Congress now going out of their way to embrace the socialist label, could the term's power as an epithet be on the wane? Maybe, but a lot of plutocrats still think it works. They attacked a modest 2021 corporate tax hike with a multimillion-dollar ad buy urging Congress to "Say No to Biden's Socialist Tax Plan."

> [THIS TAX IS BASED ON] PRINCIPLES AS *communistic, socialistic*– WHAT SHALL I CALL THEM?– *populistic* AS EVER HAVE BEEN ADDRESSED TO ANY POLITICAL ASSEMBLY IN THE WORLD.
> –JOSEPH CHOATE, 1895

For much of American history, the government mainly relied on consumption taxes on food, clothing, and other purchases, which fell heaviest on the poor and working class. In the late nineteenth century, progressives organized to make the tax code fairer and raise more from the wealthy. In 1894, during an economic depression, President Grover Cleveland (not a socialist) called for what would have been the country's first genuine income tax. It would have imposed a tax of just 2 percent on incomes above $4,000 a year—the top 1 percent at the time. Howls of complaint ensued:

> *It may be impracticable that our distinctively American experiment of individual freedom should go on.*
>
> Sen. David Hill of New York, 1894

After Congress enacted the plan, opponents challenged it in court. A lawyer arguing against the tax at the U.S. Supreme Court could hardly find the words . . .

> *[This tax is based on] principles as communistic, socialistic—what shall I call them?—populistic as ever have been addressed to any political assembly in the world.*
>
> Joseph Choate, 1895

When the justices struck the tax down as unconstitutional, plutocrats and their backers exulted:

> *The fury of ignorant class hatred has dashed itself in vain against the Constitution. . . . Thanks to the court, our government is not to be*

> *dragged into communistic warfare against rights of property and the rewards of industry.*
>
> *New York Tribune*, 1895

When President Teddy Roosevelt proposed an inheritance tax in 1906, defenders of the status quo could see where this, too, was heading:

> *[The tax gave] more encouragement to state socialism and centralization of government than all the frothy demagogues have accomplished in a quarter of a century of agitation of the muddy waters of discontent.*
>
> *Philadelphia Record*, 1906

Then, in 1909, Congress passed the Sixteenth Amendment to the Constitution, which among other things would allow the federal government to collect income taxes. The debate over ratification involved familiar arguments:

ESTATE TAXES, CARRIED TO AN *excess,* IN NO WAY DIFFER FROM THE METHODS OF THE REVOLUTIONISTS IN *Russia.* —ANDREW MELLON, 1924

> *[Taxing the rich] was supported by the Socialist party, the Populist party, and by the Democratic party with a few honorable exceptions, simply as a means of re-distributing the wealth.*
>
> Sen. Nelson Aldrich of Rhode Island, 1909

Nevertheless, the Sixteenth Amendment was ratified in early 1913. A new Democratic president, Woodrow Wilson, signed the 1913 Revenue Act, establishing the first federal income tax. Still, opponents of progressive taxation didn't back down—and after the 1917 Russian Revolution, they had a new bogeyman:

Estate taxes, carried to an excess, in no way differ from the methods of the revolutionists in Russia.

Andrew Mellon, banker, 1924

I do not believe that the Government should seek social legislation in the guise of taxation. If we are to adopt socialism, it should be presented to the people of this country as socialism, and not under the guise of a law to collect revenue.

President Calvin Coolidge, addressing a meeting of the National Tax Association, 1925

The estate tax is communistic in essence; and no party except the Socialist Party endorses the Federal estate tax.

Washington Post, 1926

It wasn't just taxes. Child labor laws, too, became part of a Soviet plot:

[A measure restricting child labor] would mean the destruction of the boys and girls of the country. This proposed amendment is fathered by Socialists, Communists and Bolshevists . . . aimed to nationalize the children of the land and bring about in this country the exact conditions that prevail in Russia.

Manufacturers' Record, 1924

[Child labor laws are] a communistic effort to nationalize children, making them primarily

DR. BUTLER ASSAILS CHILD LABOR BILL

Proposed Amendment Would Imperil Home, School, Church and Nation, He Says

The New York Times, February 3, 1934

> *responsible to the government instead of to their parents. It strikes at the home. It appears to be a definite positive plan to destroy the Republic and substitute a social democracy.*
>
> Clarence Martin, president of the American Bar Association,
>
> 1933

The socialism charge really took off during the Great Depression, especially after President Franklin Roosevelt and his congressional allies laid out the New Deal, a bold multifront program for improving life for struggling Americans:

SOCIAL SECURITY RIGHT NOW IS A *collectivist* SYSTEM. —PAUL RYAN, 2012

> *The New Deal is now undisguised state socialism.*
>
> Sen. Simeon Fess of Ohio, 1934

One component was the National Labor Relations Act (NLRA), which aimed to boost workers' bargaining power:

> *Frankly, [the NLRA] impresses me as having been written by a man who had been reading Marx on Class War, and thought all employers and employees were standing in opposite corners making faces at each other, and it is unfair to American industry.*
>
> Franklin S. Edmonds, Philadelphia Chamber of Commerce, 1934

Social Security was, of course, especially socialistic.

> *The end of democracy.*
>
> The American Liberty League, 1935

The lash of the dictator will be felt, and 25 million free American citizens will for the first time submit themselves to a fingerprint test.

Rep. Daniel Reed of New York, 1935

Too long have we introduced carelessly into the stream of our national life alien philosophies of government control and foreign ideas of repression of the individual that have no place in this land of freedom.

Philip J. Fay, U.S. Chamber of Commerce, 1936

Calling Social Security an assault on freedom still hasn't gone out of style. Here's a future Speaker of the House nearly 80 years later saying essentially the same thing:

Social Security right now is a collectivist system.

Rep. Paul Ryan of Wisconsin, 2012

Attempts to create a minimum wage, too, have always been socialism. Or worse:

This would be communism with a vengeance.

Ben W. Hooper, former Tennessee governor, 1923

No greater calamity could befall the wage earners of the country than to have the legislative power to fix wages upheld. . . . It will logically, if persisted in, end in social disorder and revolution.

Judge Josiah Van Orsdel, 1923

The Fair Labor Standards Act of 1938 might have been even more vilified:

> *[It] will destroy small industry. . . . [These ideas are] the product of those whose thinking is rooted in an alien philosophy and who are bent upon the destruction of our whole constitutional system and the setting up of a red-labor communistic despotism upon the ruins of our Christian civilization.*
>
> Rep. Edward Cox of Georgia, 1938

THE CREEPING SOCIALISM BEGINS AT THE *$5.05* LEVEL.
—ERIC MUND, 1993

With the rise of fascism in Germany and Italy, opponents had other scary-sounding epithets, too:

> *[The Fair Labor Standards Act] constitutes a step in the direction of communism, bolshevism, fascism, and Nazism.*
>
> National Association of Manufacturers, 1938

Vandenberg Fears "Fascist" Wage Bill

The New York Times, June 6, 1937

> *[It] will lead to compulsory arbitration in labor relations . . . as we are driven closer and closer to the centralized authoritarian State, with its tyranny of oppressive government-blessed monopolies.*
>
> Sen. Arthur Vandenberg of Michigan, 1937

Even decades later, conservatives were still calling the minimum wage socialism:

> *The Federal wage and hour law is one of the most vicious, anti-democratic pieces of legislation that has ever been perpetrated on the American public.*
>
> Lewis Manufacturing Co., Klamath Falls, Oregon, 1960

> *The creeping socialism begins at the $5.05 level.*
>
> Eric Mund, Burger King franchise owner, 1993

> *Slowly but surely they're taking away your liberty to mutually make employment decisions. I dare say that's socialism. It's government paternalism at its worst.*
>
> Mark Wilson, The Heritage Foundation, 1997

Another thing that's socialism? Civil rights. One segregationist southern governor made the link in denouncing Rev. Dr. Martin Luther King Jr. and other civil rights activists:

> *These "four horsemen" of racial agitation have brought tension, disturbance, strife, and violence in their advancement of the Communist doctrine of "racial nationalism."*
>
> Gov. Ross Barnett of Mississippi, 1963

After civil rights workers James Chaney, Andrew Goodman, and Michael Schwerner went missing in Mississippi during the Freedom Summer of 1964, one of the state's senators suggested it might all be part of a Red-driven hoax:

> *[There is a] Communist conspiracy to further or to participate in the invasion of Mississippi.*
>
> Sen. James Eastland of
> Mississippi, 1964

EASTLAND LABELS RIGHTS DRIVE "RED"
Sees a Hoax in Mississippi Disappearance of 3 Men
The New York Times, July 23, 1964

Not long after, of course, the activists' bodies were found. They had been murdered by white supremacists.

Protecting the health and safety of workers on the job—or even compensating workers for illnesses they'd already developed—is also, apparently, an assault on freedom. A West Virginia bill to benefit miners who'd contracted black lung, a disease estimated to afflict 100,000 miners nationally, was described as:

> *Galloping socialism in its purest form.*
> Quinn Morton, West Virginia Coal Association, 1969

Agitation to pass a federal law protecting workers in the 1960s generated a frenzy of "police state" claims:

> *The Act broadly authorizes the Secretary to grab any police powers in the occupational health and safety fields that are now held by states. State safety officials could be forced to report directly to the federal Secretary when he says so.*
>
> U.S. Chamber of Commerce, 1968

> *There is no evidence, in our opinion, which requires or justifies the imposition of a Federal police system for safety upon industry at this time.*
>
> Wallace Smith, American Mutual Insurance Alliance, 1968

Nevertheless, President Richard Nixon signed the Occupational Safety and Health Act (OSHA), along with legislation establishing the Environmental Protection Agency, the Clean Air and Water Acts, the Equal Employment Opportunity Act, the Endangered Species Act and more. Nixon's comparative liberalism, early in his first term, showed the broad consensus that existed about the need to protect workers and the environment. But the backlash was looming.

For some reason (feminists have a few thoughts), the 1971 Comprehensive Child Development Act went too far for Nixon. The bill would have created federally funded, locally administered child care centers, to provide education, nutrition, and healthcare services. Slots would be available on a sliding scale basis to accommodate the growing ranks of middle-class working mothers, avoiding the stigma of "welfare."

Meanwhile, Nixon's legendary far-right advisor Pat Buchanan warned that the measure would lead to the "Sovietization of American children." Nixon left that flourish out of his veto statement but kept the sentiment:

> *The CDA would commit the vast moral authority of the national government to the side of communal approaches to childrearing over the family-centered approach.*
>
> Richard Nixon, 1971

THIS SOCIALIST DIKTAT TAKES FEEL-GOOD POLITICS TO A NEW LEVEL . . . THE BASIC ARGUMENT FOR THIS *socialist propaganda* IS THE NECESSITY FOR BIG BROTHER TO SUBSIDIZE AN ARMY OF BREASTFEEDING *single mothers.* —STEVEN LONEGAN, 2007

Efforts to support working women often wound up painted red—or pink? Here's how one lawmaker described an early version of the Family and Medical Leave Act (FMLA):

> *This disturbing trend is nothing short of Europeanization—a polite term for socialism.*
>
> Rep. Cass Ballenger of North Carolina, 1987

After the FMLA was signed into law in 1993, one up-and-coming Republican lamented:

> *America's business owners are a resilient bunch, but let there be no doubt, [the Family Medical Leave Act] will be the demise of some. And as that occurs, the light of freedom will grow dimmer.*
>
> Rep. John Boehner of Ohio, 1993

Since then, some states have tried to go beyond unpaid leave, which low-income parents often can't afford to take, to require businesses or government to offer paid leave. Those efforts have often gotten the same treatment—with some outright misogyny thrown in:

This socialist diktat takes feel-good politics to a new level . . . the basic argument for this socialist propaganda is the necessity for Big Brother to subsidize an army of breastfeeding single mothers.

Steven Lonegan, mayor of Bogota, New Jersey, and executive director of Americans for Prosperity, 2007

OUR SOCIALIST PRESIDENTS

Since as far back as FDR, every Democratic president's policies or agenda—and in many cases, they themselves—have been blasted as socialist.

Roosevelt is a socialist, not a Democrat.

Rep. Robert Rich of Pennsylvania, 1935

[Present Harry Truman's policies] would commit us irrevocably to a socialistic state from which there is no retreat.

Sen. Harry Byrd of Virginia, 1950

President John F. Kennedy, a consummate cold warrior, was branded a communist hours before his death:

BYRD TIES TRUMAN TO SOCIALIST DRIFT

Tells Political Scientists That Policies Sap Free Enterprise to Point of "No Retreat"

The New York Times, April 27, 1950

Mr. President, because of your socialist tendencies and because of your surrender to communism, I hold you in complete contempt.

> Sign greeting Kennedy in Dallas,
> |November 22, 1963

Senator Barry Goldwater seems to have agreed. Here's what he wrote to Lyndon Johnson, when he heard he was considering an offer to be Kennedy's running mate:

It is . . . incredible to try to understand how you are going to try to embrace the socialist platform of your party.

> Barry Goldwater, 1960

Of course, Johnson was pretty much a socialist, too:

[Johnson's Great Society program came] close enough to socialism to cause an American tragedy.

> Amity Schlaes, conservative writer, 2019

Many people saw Presidents Jimmy Carter and Bill Clinton as southern moderates, but to the plutocrats and their allies, they were socialists as well:

[If Carter is elected] what happens then is the coming of Christian Socialism to America.

> Clare Booth Luce,
> conservative writer, 1976

As for Clinton:

The man is a socialist.

> State Rep. John Becker of Ohio, 1993

But few people were more socialist than President Barack Obama:

Obama's a hardcore socialist, and he's marvelous at pretending to be something other than that, but that is what I believe he truly is, a hardcore socialist. He's scary to me.

> Energy magnate and right-wing
> philanthropist David Koch, 2011

And we can't forget Joe Biden:

> Don't ask me to get inside the mind of a liberal, progressive, socialist, Marxist like President Biden.
>> Sen. Ron Johnson of Wisconsin, 2021

> The $3.5 trillion Biden plan isn't socialism, it's Marxism.
>> Sen. Marco Rubio of Florida, 2021

> [Biden's Build Back Better plan is] meant to be a Trojan Horse for permanent socialism.
>> Sen. Minority Leader Mitch McConnell, 2021

In fact, Biden had the pithiest rejoinder to the socialist tag.

"I beat the socialist," he said in an interview during his 2020 campaign, referring to Senator Bernie Sanders, who calls himself a democratic socialist. "That's how I got the nomination. Do I look like a socialist?"

But it was Truman who came up with the best comeback of all, while campaigning for Adlai Stevenson in 1952:

> Socialism is what they called Social Security.
> Socialism is what they called farm price supports.
> Socialism is what they called bank deposit insurance.
> Socialism is what they called the growth of free and independent labor organizations.
> Socialism is their name for almost anything that helps all the people.

C·A·S·E S·T·U·D·Y

HEALTHCARE

For the past 80 years, activists have been fighting to expand access to healthcare. Arrayed against them has been the power of industry: Doctors, some hospitals, insurance companies, and pharmaceutical giants have been invested in the lucrative status quo. Efforts to challenge their power and profits have often inspired charges of socialism.

Of course, we've never had socialized medicine in the United States. Even Medicare and Medicaid—overwhelmingly popular programs that together have provided health insurance to hundreds of millions of Americans who might not otherwise have been able to obtain it—are designed to leave the private healthcare provider market intact. Yet, our so-called free-market healthcare system costs approximately twice as much per capita per year as government-run healthcare systems like those of Canada, Germany, and Australia, with worse health outcomes.

When FDR tried to include healthcare for the elderly in a version of the Social Security Act, it was one of the few provisions that failed completely—thanks in part to a concerted campaign by industry and its allies.

> *The association has for years been a foe of sickness insurance plans. Such plans are a step toward socialized medicine.*
> American Medical Association (AMA), 1935

As the Cold War began, the rhetoric about federal efforts to promote health insurance heated up, starting with Truman's modest plan:

The New York Times, February 16, 1935

Doctors Meet on "Peril" in Security Plans
Illness Insurance Moves Stir Profession

I considered it socialism. It is to my mind the most socialistic measure this Congress has ever had before it.

Sen. Robert Taft of Ohio, 1946

Would socialized medicine lead to socialization of other phases of American life? Lenin thought so. He declared: "Socialized medicine is the keystone to the arch of the Socialist state."

AMA, 1949

Early efforts at what eventually became Medicare, begun under President Kennedy, helped galvanize the modern right-wing movement—and Ronald Reagan's political career. In 1961, the AMA produced a recording, "Ronald Reagan Speaks Out Against Socialized Medicine," featuring Reagan six years before he would become governor of California.

Ronald Reagan recorded an anti-Medicare message for the American Medical Association, which was distributed as an LP.

A.M.A. CRITICIZES MEDICARE IN AD
Says It Would Be "Beginning of Socialized Medicine"
The New York Times, June 9, 1965

[If Medicare legislation passes,] we will awake to find that we have socialism. . . . One of the traditional methods of imposing statism or socialism has been by way of medicine. . . . If you don't do this, one of these days you and I are going to spend our sunset years telling our children and our children's children what it was like in America when men were free.

Ronald Reagan, 1961

Reagan continued his crusade in a 1964 speech endorsing Goldwater, a staunch Medicare foe, for president:

> *Realize that the doctor's fight against socialized medicine is your fight. We can't socialize the doctors without socializing the patients.*
>
> Ronald Reagan, 1964

When the Medicare debate began for real during Johnson's Great Society campaign in 1965, the Red Scare language continued:

> *It is socialism. It moves the country in a direction which is not good for anyone, whether they be young or old. It charts a course from which there will be no turning back.*
>
> Sen. Carl Curtis of Nebraska, 1965

Senator Ted Kennedy's 1970's push for some form of universal healthcare inspired the same argument:.

> *Some people think that people are entitled to health care as a matter of right, whether they work or not. This is just as absurd as saying that food, clothes, and shelter are a matter of*

May 26, 1994. A Herblock Cartoon, © The Herb Block Foundation.

right—one step further than that is a revolutionary system bordering on communism.

Dr. Edward R. Annis,
former AMA president, 1971

Same with President Clinton's plans for a health care overhaul. His proposal never even received serious congressional debate, in part because opponents labeled it creeping socialism from the outset:

[Clinton's healthcare proposal] resembles long-standing plans by congressional Democrats to impose a version of socialized medicine in America.

Orange County Register, 1992

We have arrived at socialized medicine in America. . . . Our politics and economy will never again be the same.

Robert J. Samuelson, *Washington Post*
columnist, 1993

Republicans trashed the doomed Clinton plan not only as a socialist plot, but something Hillary Clinton cooked up, also known as "Hillarycare":

[The Clintons' healthcare initiative is] washed-over old-time bureaucratic liberalism, or centralized bureaucratic socialism.

Republican whip Newt Gingrich, 1993

Same with Senator Hillary Clinton's reform proposals as a candidate for president in 2008:

The last thing we need is Hillarycare. The last thing we need is socialized medicine.

Mitt Romney, former Republican presidential
candidate, 2007

When you hear Democrats in particular talk about single-mandated health care, universal health care, what they're talking about is socialized medicine.

Rudy Giuliani, former mayor of New York
City, 2007

One of President Clinton's top accomplishments was enacting a federally subsidized State Children's Health Insurance Program (SCHIP) in 1997, which provides health insurance for working-class families whose incomes are too high to qualify for Medicaid. Despite the sponsorship of Senator Orrin Hatch of

Utah, a conservative Republican (along with Senator Ted Kennedy), opponents still cried socialism:

> *[The GOP] must decide soon where they stand on the issue of socialized medicine. President Clinton threw down the gauntlet in his State of the Union address, when he proposed guaranteeing health insurance for at least half of the 10 million American children who have none.*
>
> Tony Snow, conservative columnist and future
> White House press secretary, 1997

> *[I am] confident that Congress will pass the Kennedy-Hatch KidCare bill, a first step toward . . . single-payer socialized medicine.*
>
> Phyllis Schlafly,
> legendary conservative activist, 1997

When Hatch and Kennedy moved to reauthorize and expand the plan in 2007, it was still "socialized medicine":

> *The Children's Health Insurance Program has given Democrats a wide-open door for socialized medicine. The door was left open by Republicans,*

who were in the majority when we passed the original legislation in 1997.

> Rep. Jack Kingston of Georgia, 2007

Congress passed the legislation—and President George W. Bush signed it. That made no difference to the rhetoric:

> *[The Democrats'] vision for the future: socialized medicine and Washington-run health care.*
>
> Rep. Pete Sessions of Texas, 2007

Of course, everything that Barack Obama wanted to do equaled socialism to many Republicans:

> *Ask why Barack Obama wants to make us all wards of the state, with state health care. Is this a good moment to embrace 20th Century Socialism Lite, even if we are facing a year or two of belt tightening? Shouldn't the future be freer, with less state interference in our lives?*
>
> *National Review*, 2008

When Obama proposed an SCHIP expansion, it was as socialist as Bush and Clinton's:

> *This will increase burdens on taxpayers and take a significant step toward socialized medicine.*
>
> Sen. Jim DeMint of South Carolina, 2009

Of course, Obama's Affordable Care Act met with more Red Scare quotes:

> This is the crown jewel of socialism. . . . It's unconstitutional.
>
> Rep. Michele Bachmann of Minnesota, 2009

> We are treading dangerously close to bureaucratic intervention in the exam room and I will not support any measure that leads to socialized medicine.
>
> Rep. John Fleming of Louisiana, 2010

> [The healthcare bill is a] headlong rush into socialism. . . . We will not stand for the Obama-Pelosi-Reid hijacking of our freedom and democracy so they can impose their socialist "utopia" of higher taxes, restricted access, inferior quality, and

OBAMACARE
Will Suck the Life
Out of the Economy
CNBC, JUNE 26, 2014

> deadly inefficiency on the best health care system in the world.
>
> Michael Steele, chairman of the Republican National Committee, 2010

Obama signed into law what was formally known as the Patient Protection and Affordable Care Act, but widely hailed or derided as "Obamacare," on March 23, 2010. Since then, the number of uninsured Americans has dropped by nearly 18 million. We are still living without socialism, or even socialized medicine.

CONCLUSION

NOW WHAT?

It's no exaggeration to say that the century-plus of corrosive corporate lies we expose here helped lead to our fractured "post-fact" society, where everyone has their own "truth"—and the truth purveyed by the wealthy and powerful prevails far too much of the time. As we've seen, it's no kind of truth—just a craftily spun web of lies and deceit finessed over time, spread ever more widely, to justify ever increasing wealth, profits and power—the suffering of others be damned. This brazen crusade to spread lies and deny truth is now corroding our democracy. Corporate elites and their allies perfected a rhetorical style that relies on deception, fear and demonizing their opponents. Those tactics are now used to undermine faith not just in government, but in the electoral process that allows Americans to govern themselves.

We live in a time of remarkable opportunity—and peril. Once again, movements of consumers, workers, students, civil rights advocates, climate activists, and others have come together to demand a more just society, with equal opportunity for all. Too often, they're being thwarted or limited by the same old forces of wealth and reaction that met similar demands for change throughout American history, using the same old deceitful, self-serving stories.

A threadbare social safety net exposed by the disruptions of a deadly pandemic? Not a problem.

Dramatic healthcare inequities? The free market can fix it. The widespread availability of guns leading to tens of thousands of avoidable deaths per year? It's not our fault—it's your fault. Increasing taxes on the uber-wealthy? It'll kill jobs. Raising the federal minimum wage for the first time in a decade and a half? You'll only make things worse. Universal pre-kindergarten? Socialism!

Recognize the pattern?

It's also worth noting, in the legislative skirmishes of the early 2020s, the only public investment the forces of wealth supported was old-fashioned "infrastructure"—using the government to build or modernize roads, bridges, railways, ports and airports; to fix crumbling water and sewage pipes; to fund broadband service just the way government once funded electrification projects, and other investments essential to commerce. This spending is badly needed, to be sure. But, this is the kind of "socialism" plutocrats like—the kind that lets them freeload off the rest of us to maximize their profits, while crucial investments in public health, safety, and education are deemed unaffordable or downright unwise.

They are shameless—but it's our job to work harder to shame them. And stop them.

How do we do that? Reading this book is a start: knowledge really is power. Once you see how ridiculous, and ridiculously consistent, these plutocrats' stories are, you'll never be able to unsee it. You'll start to marvel every time there's a debate about solving a national—or global—problem. Next time the minimum wage is debated in Washington, in cities, or in states; as we tackle climate change, create a broader safety net for families, or strive for more progressive taxes on the uber-wealthy: you will greet the repetitive counter-arguments with the ridicule and mockery they deserve.

Now you know how to name them, blame them, and shame them. Here are some specific ways to promote change:

When you see one of these industry-serving storylines, first ask a few questions. Who's telling the story, and how do they stand to benefit from the status quo? It might not be an oil company report, editorial, or spokesperson making the claim that climate change is a hoax. It might be an oil company-funded think tank, industry association, political group, or even an elected official.

Then ask yourself: Where have I heard that before?

Are they opposing a proposed environmental regulation? If so, check the bizarre arguments used to oppose the Clean Air Act. Is it the minimum wage? Look back at what happened every time the minimum wage was increased. (Here's a shortcut: The nation's fast-food industry would have died if all those cry-wolf stories about how they couldn't possibly afford higher wages came true. Instead, it continues to thrive.)

Talk back!

If the industry-serving storyline is by a news reporter or opinion writer, contact them and explain what they got wrong. If it's by an academic, don't be intimidated. Ask about their research methods, their funding—and again, explain what they got wrong. If it's sponsored by a department at your alma mater, the good old University of Sorry, We Sold Out to Business, explain why you're unhappy and what you plan to do about it. And if it's purveyed by a politician who represents you—from the local school board to the Senate—explain what they got wrong and how you plan to organize to vote them out of office until they stop telling corporate lies and start telling the truth for working people.

Commit to telling better stories.

For instance, that consumers, not the wealthy, are the real job creators. When they have more money in their pockets, they buy more food, clothing, homes, household goods, eat at restaurants, even take vacations—and all of that creates jobs throughout the economy because when businesses have more customers, they hire more workers. Or that unions helped build the American middle class and must be strengthened. That higher tax rates also powered the building of that middle class—and must do so again.

Vote—with your ballot, and with your dollar.

Don't support politicians who are in the pocket of industry. Examine who's funding them. Look out for candidates—both incumbents and newcomers—who have pledged to make life fairer and easier for the rest of us and are not funded by special interests (unsurprisingly, those things go together). Don't support corporations that are purveying these lies—and also, of course, pursuing the kinds of greedy, socially and environmentally destructive policies that make these deceitful stories essential to their bottom line.

This is just a start. You'll have other ideas. Thank you for reading—and for caring about the truth.

ACKNOWLEDGMENTS

THIS BOOK IS THE RESULT OF A PROJECT LONG IN THE making.

Peter Dreier, professor at Occidental College and a prolific writer, first began writing about how business would claim the sky would fall (the "Chicken Little" syndrome) if the laws and protections we now take for granted would become law. With the book's co-author Donald Cohen, Dreier was a key partner in developing the original project idea and generating tons of case studies and articles. He wrote many of the original articles in what we went on to call "The Cry Wolf Project," where much of this research was housed.

Bob Shull, during his time as a program officer at the Public Welfare Foundation, saw the potential of the idea and offered a grant to get it going. The project would not have happened without his support.

Jake Blumgart was the Cry Wolf Project's dogged researcher and writer who scoured the literature, found quotes, and put them into context for current battles.

Under the leadership of professor of history Joe McCartin, a three-month fellowship at the Kalmanovitz Institute at Georgetown University gave Donald the time, a Georgetown office, and full access to research facilities of the university to delve deeper. Joe's intellectual guidance and support was crucial in developing the analysis that is now the core structure of this book.

As we got closer to turning this set of great ideas into a book, we knew we needed an ace researcher. We found Zachary Roth, author of the epic *The Great Suppression: Voting Rights, Corporate Cash, and the Conservative Assault on Democracy*. Zack became more than a researcher: he edited, he rewrote, he found whole new areas of corporate chicanery we could debunk and ridicule. This project became more epic as he pushed us to be more ambitious. It would not be what it is without him.

This book might not have happened without the enthusiastic support of The New Press editor Julie Enszer, who we are so thankful to have had the chance to work with. Her steady and constant presence, guidance, and critical engagement with the ideas and how to present them made this the high-quality book that it is.

We also want to thank the many leaders, researchers, and advocates for a healthy and fair society who helped us understand the issues and opened up their archives. And for their continuing dedication to making the country—and the world—a better, fairer and more humane place. We have cited them in our endnotes; there are too many, thankfully, to name here.

David Goldstein and Paul Constant at Civic Ventures lent their brilliant writing and editing minds to this manuscript. They saw things that the authors were too close to observe, and deftly fixed them.

Finally, and absolutely not least, Annie Fadely at Civic Ventures was our guiding hand, kept us on deadline, and solved every problem and roadblock along the way. Her intellectual contribution to the book was essential. The world would be a better place if Annie was in charge.

NOTES

Preface

"Minimum wage opponents continue to deride": Noam Scheiber (@noamscheiber), "California makes itself a guinea pig in a massive and risky minimum wage experiment," Twitter, March 29, 2016.

"Raising minimum wage risky": *Herald Leader* headline: Letter to the Editor, *Lexington Herald Leader*, April 1, 2016.

"Raising minimum wage hurts low-skill workers": "Editorial: Raising Minimum Wage Hurts Low-Skill Workers," *The Detroit News*, April 5, 2016.

"Even left-leaning economists say it's a gamble": Timothy B. Lee, "California Just Passed a $15 Minimum Wage. Even Left-Leaning Economists Say It's a Gamble," *Vox*, March 31, 2016.

"Federal minimum wage has been raised 22 times": U.S. Department of Labor, "History of Changes to the Minimum Wage Law," www.dol.gov/agencies/whd/minimum-wage/history

"Study after peer-reviewed study has found little or no correlation": David Card and Alan B. Krueger, "Minimum Wages and Employment: A Case Study of the Fast Food Industry in New Jersey and Pennsylvania," *National Bureau of Economic Research*, 1993, www.nber.org/papers/w4509; Restaurant Opportunities Center United, *Better Wages, Better Tips: Restaurants Flourish with One Fair Wage* (New York: Restaurant Opportunities Center United, 2018); Sylvia Allegretto and Carl Nadler, *Tipped Wage Effects on Earnings and Employment in Full-Service Restaurants* (Berkeley, CA: Institute for Research on Labor and Employment, 2015); Anna Godoey and Michael Reich, *Minimum Wage Effects in Low-Wage Areas* (Berkeley, CA: Institute for Research on Labor and Employment, 2019); Paul J. Wolfson and Dale Belman, *15 Years of Research on U.S. Employment and the Minimum Wage* (Hanover, NH: Tuck School of Business, 2016); Doruk Cengiz et al., "The Effect of Minimum Wages on Low-Wage Jobs," *Quarterly Journal of Economics*, 134, no. 3 (2019): 1405–1454, doi:10.1093/qje/qjz014

Introduction

"Far fewer Americans die on the roads": National Safety Council, "Car Crash Deaths and Rates," injuryfacts.nsc.org /motor-vehicle/historical-fatality-trends/deaths-and-rates

"fewer workers are injured, sickened, or killed on the job": David Michaels and Jordan Barab, "The Occupational Safety and Health Administration at 50: Protecting Workers in a Changing Economy," *American Journal of Public Health*, 110, no. 5 (January 19, 2020): 631–635, doi:10.2105/AJPH.2020.305597

"Our kids breathe cleaner air and drink cleaner water": U.S. Environmental Protection Agency, "Our Nation's Air," https://gispub.epa.gov/air/trendsreport/2021/#home; U.S. Environmental Protection Agency, "EPA at 50: Progress in Providing Safe Drinking Water," February 18, 2020, www.epa.gov /newsreleases/epa-50-progress-providing-safe-drinking-water

"We've dramatically cut poverty": U.S. Census Bureau, Figure 8: Number in Poverty and Poverty Rate, 1959–2020, www.census.gov/content/dam/Census/library/visualizations /2021/demo/p60-273/Figure8.pdf

"especially among the elderly": Zhe Li and Joseph Dalaker, "Poverty Among the Population Aged 65 and Older," Congressional Research Service, crsreports.congress.gov/product /pdf/R/R45791/6

"steadily expanded access to healthcare": Kaiser Family Foundation, "History of Health Reform in the U.S.," www.kff.org/wp -content/uploads/2011/03/5-02-13-history-of-health-reform .pdf

"We've made it much harder for businesses or government to single out women, people of color, and LGBTQ Americans for unfair treatment": The Civil Rights Act of 1964, as well as state laws barring anti-LGBTQ discrimination.

"left out of this prosperity, often by design": Council of Economic Advisers for the President's Initiative on Race, *Changing America: Indicators of Social and Economic Well-Being by Race and Hispanic Origin*, September 1998, www.govinfo.gov /content/pkg/GPO-EOP-CHANGINGAMERICA/pdf/GPO -EOP-CHANGINGAMERICA.pdf

"In the years from 1947 to 1973, under presidents of both parties, real wages rose by 81 percent, while wages for the top 1 percent rose by less than half of that": Paul Krugman, "Wages, Wealth, and Politics," *The New York Times*, April 18, 2006.

"'The federal government fought a war on poverty, and poverty won'": President Ronald Reagan, "Address Before a Joint Session of Congress on the State of the Union" (January 25, 1988), The American Presidency Project, www.presidency.ucsb.edu /documents/address-before-joint-session-congress-the-state -the-union-0

"Income inequality increased by 20 percent between 1980 and 2016" and *"The top 1 percent's share"*: Juliana Menasce Horowitz, Ruth Igielnik, and Rakesh Kochhar, "Trends in Income and Wealth Inequality," Pew Research Center, January 9, 2020, www.pewresearch.org/social-trends/2020/01/09/trends-in -income-and-wealth-inequality

"A RAND Corporation study": Nick Hanauer and David M. Rolf, "The Top 1% of Americans Have Taken $50 Trillion from the Bottom 90%—and That's Made the U.S. Less Secure," *Time*, September 14, 2020.

"The net worth of a typical white family": Horowitz, Igielnik, and Kochhar, "Trends in Income and Wealth Inequality."

"median wealth of a Latino household": Dedrick Asante-Muhammad, Alexandra Perez, and Jamie Buell, "Racial Wealth Snapshot: Latino Americans," *National Community Reinvestment Coalition*, September 17, 2021.

"Safety is good business": "OSHA—Crying Need for Fair Play," Chamber of Commerce newsletter, June 1973.

"In the Jim Crow South, those places flourished": Angela Jill Cooley, *"To Live and Dine in Dixie: The Evolution of Urban Food Culture in the Jim Crow South"* (Athens: University of Georgia Press, 2015).

"A series of massive corporate tax cuts has done little to spur jobs": Emily Horton, "The Legacy of the 2001 and 2003 'Bush' Tax Cuts," Center on Budget and Policy Priorities, October 23, 2017, www.cbpp.org/research/federal-tax/the-legacy-of-the -2001-and-2003-bush-tax-cuts; Scott Horsley, "After Two Years, Trump Tax Cuts Have Failed to Deliver on GOP's Promises," National Public Radio, December 20, 2019, www .npr.org/2019/12/20/789540931/2-years-later-trump-tax -cuts-have-failed-to-deliver-on-gops-promises

"decades-long economic inequality and the Covid-19 pandemic have exposed a badly frayed safety net": Catherine Albiston and Catherine L. Fisk, "Blog: Covid-19 Reveals Gaping Holes in U.S. Social Safety Net," *California Law Review*, May 2020, https://www.californialawreview.org/covid-19-holes-in-us -social-safety-net/

1: It's Not a Problem

"It is but the natural course of mining events": William Graebner, *Coal-Mining Safety in the Progressive Period: The Political Economy of Reform* (Lexington: University of Kentucky Press, 1976), 73.

"There is absolutely no proof that cigarettes": Comprehensive Smoking Prevention Education Act: Hearing Before the Subcommittee on Health and Environment of the Committee on Energy and Commerce, 2d Sess. on H.R. 5653 and H.R. 4957, 97th Cong., pt. 1 (March 5, 11, and 12, 1982), 390.

"What the hell is going on with global warming?": Michael Burke, "Trump Calls for Global Warming to 'Come Back' Amid Winter Storm," *The Hill*, January 28, 2019.

"As a class, I say it boldly; there is not a happier, more contented race": John Henry Hammond, *Remarks of Mr. Hammond, of South Carolina, on the Question of Receiving Petitions for the Abolition of Slavery in the District of Columbia. Delivered in the House of Representatives, February 1, 1836* (Washington, DC: D. Green, 1836), 11–12, 15.

"Never before has the black race of Central Africa": John C. Calhoun, "Slavery a Positive Good," speech, February 6, 1837, teachingamericanhistory.org/document/slavery-a-positive -good.

"The Negro slaves of the South are the happiest": George Fitzhugh, *Cannibals All! Or Slaves Without Masters* (Richmond, VA: A. Morris, 1857), 278.

"who would otherwise be idle": Alexander Hamilton, *Report on the Subject of Manufactures* [5 December 1791], U.S. National Archives, founders.archives.gov/documents/Hamilton/01-10 -02-0001-0007

"In 1900, an estimated 18 percent of children": James L. Roark et al., *The American Promise: A History of the United States* (Boston: Bedford/St. Martin's, 2020).

"I have seen children working in factories": New York Factory Investigating Commission, *Second Report of the Factory Investigating Commission, 1913* (Albany, NY: J.B. Lyon Company, 1913), 1,961.

"We do not ourselves approve of the glass house or the cotton mill": Alan Derickson, "Making Human Junk: Child Labor as a Health Issue in the Progressive Era," *American Journal of Public Health*, 82, no. 9 (September 1992).

"The pictures which your committee has published as representative": "Denies Child Labor Tales; Southern Editor Tells Reformers to Mind Their Own Business," *The New York Times*, January 7, 1915.

New York Times headline: "Denies Child Labor Tales."

"In 1920, for the first time, a near majority of high school-age students remained in school": David M. Kennedy, *Freedom from Fear: The American People in Depression and War, 1929–1945* (New York: Oxford University Press, 1999).

"twice in recent years struck down as unconstitutional": *Hammer v. Dagenhart*, 247 US 251, 1918; *Bailey v. Drexel Furniture*, 259 US 20, 1922.

"That led Congress in 1924 to pass a constitutional amendment": Jessie Kratz, "Unratified Amendments: Regulating Child Labor," *Pieces of History* (blog), U.S. National Archives, March 24, 2020.

"Our investigations thus far have indicated that the home and farm work": John Edward Garrett, "The Defeat of the Child Labor Amendment, 1924–1925" (master's thesis, University of Arizona, 1964), repository.arizona.edu/handle/10150/347476

"The opposition campaign succeeded": Kratz, "Unratified Amendments: Regulating Child Labor."

"In Iowa, we understand there is dignity in work": Kaanita Iyer, "Iowa Governor Signs Bill to Loosen Child Labor Laws," CNN, May 27, 2023, https://www.cnn.com/2023/05/26/politics/iowa-child-labor-law-kim-reynolds/index.html

"Upton Sinclair's best-selling 1906 novel The Jungle": Christopher Wilson, "The Making of a Best Seller, 1906," *The New York Times*, December 22, 1985.

"added momentum to the push for the Meat Inspection Act of 1906": David Moss and Marc Campasano, "*The Jungle* and the Debate Over Federal Meat Inspection in 1906," Harvard Business School Case 716-045, February 2016 (revised October 2017).

"It makes business sense to have them clean": Philip J. Hilts, *Protecting America's Health: The FDA, Business, and One Hundred Years of Regulation* (Chapel Hill: University of North Carolina Press, 2004), 44.

"Meat canned five years ago is just as good": Meat Inspection Act of 1906: Hearings Before the Committee on Agriculture . . . on the So-Called "Beveridge Amendment" to the Agricultural Appropriation Bill (H.R. 18537) as Passed by the Senate, May 25, 1906, House Committee on Agriculture, 59th Cong., 5th Sess. 231 (1906).

"It's rather asinine to think cotton fiber is hazardous": Joan Mower, "Governors to Debate Cotton Dust Rules," *Sarasota Herald Tribune*, September 19, 1978.

"Industrial waste is not a menace to public health": Hearings Before a Subcommittee of the Committee on Public Works, U.S. Senate, 80th Cong., 1st Sess. on S. 418 (1947).

"water that comes out of our plants . . . in many cases . . . is purer": Art Pine, "DuPont's Irving S. Shapiro: Summing Up a Lifetime in Business," *The Washington Post*, February 8, 1981.

"The Ford engineering staff, although mindful": Letter to Los Angeles County Supervisor Kenneth Hahn [March 3, 1953], submitted in Hearings of the U.S. Senate Committee on Public Works, Subcommittee on Air and Water Pollution (1967), 158.

"no scientific evidence showing a threat to health from automotive emissions": Jack Doyle, *Taken for a Ride: Detroit's Big Three and the Politics of Pollution* (New York: Four Walls Eight Windows, 2000), 91–92.

"Shoulder harnesses [seat belts] and head rests are complete wastes of money": Environmental Working Group, "Blind Spot: The Big Three's Attack on the Global Warming Treaty," November 20, 1997.

"no positive proof of a causal relationship between the use of thalidomide": Hearings Before the Antitrust Subcommittee (Subcommittee No. 5) of the Committee on the Judiciary, House of Representatives, 87th Cong., 2d Sess. on H.R. 6245, 653 (May 17, 18, 23, and 24, 1962).

"Appeal to the doctor's ego": "Merrell Sales Effort," Interagency Coordination in Drug Research and Regulation, *Hearings Before the United States Senate Committee on Government Operations, Subcommittee on Reorganization and International Organizations*, 87th and 88th Congs., pts. 4–6 (1963), 1,918.

"By 1962, '10,000 children, mostly in Europe, had been born with thalidomide-induced birth defects'": Carl Zimmer, "Answers Begin to Emerge on How Thalidomide Caused Defects," *The New York Times*, March 15, 2010.

"the Food and Drug Administration refused to approve thalidomide": U.S. Food and Drug Administration, "Frances Oldham Kelsey: Medical Reviewer Famous for Averting a Public Health Tragedy," www.fda.gov/about-fda/fda-history-exhibits/frances-oldham-kelsey-medical-reviewer-famous-averting-public-health-tragedy

"Even if it [the Equal Pay Act] could be administered and enforced, no evidence": Cynthia Harrison, *On Account of Sex: The Politics of Women's Issues, 1945-1968* (Berkeley: University of California Press, 1989), 99.

"Emotional appeals about working families": Nick Littlefield and David Nexon, *Lion of the Senate: When Ted Kennedy Rallied the Democrats in a GOP Congress* (New York: Simon & Schuster, 2015), 362.

"There have been no reports of illness or death which can be attributed to pesticides": Federal Pesticide Control Act of 1971: Hearings Before the House Committee on Agriculture, House of Representatives, 92nd Cong., 150 (February–March 1971).

"Pesticides Defended; Public Is Said": L.S. Hitchner, "Pesticides Defended; Public Is Said to Have Protection from Hazards at Misuse," *The New York Times*, August 16, 1961.

"We are disappointed that they have chosen to continue": Marian Burros, "High Pesticide Levels Seen in U.S. Food," *The New York Times*, February 19, 1999.

"Lead helps to guard your health": Gerald Markowitz and David Rosner, *Deceit and Denial: The Deadly Politics of Industrial Pollution* (Berkeley: University of California Press, 2002), 82.

"The Dutch Boy's Hobby ad": U.S. National Medical Library, *The Dutch Boy's Hobby: A Paint Book for Girls and Boys*, www.nlm.nih.gov/exhibition/thisleadiskillingus/collection

"There is no evidence that lead in the atmosphere, from autos or any other source, poses a health hazard": David Bird, "Industry Defends Lead in Gasoline," *The New York Times*, September 25, 1970.

"The people in this room have the same amount of lead in their blood": Don Smith, "Orange County Sets 1975 Ban on Sale of Gasoline with Lead," *Los Angeles Times*, October 28, 1971.

"estimated to cause at least 674,000 deaths worldwide": Perry Gottesfeld and Johnson Ongking, "Eliminating Lead Paint Would Save Millions of Lives," *San Jose Mercury-News*, November 28, 2018.

"projected to prevent more than 1.2 million premature deaths": United Nations Environment Programme, "Era of Leaded Petrol Over, Eliminating a Major Threat to Human and Planetary Health," press release, August 30, 2021, www.unep.org/news-and-stories/press-release/era-leaded-petrol-over-eliminating-major-threat-human-and-planetary

"Bush signs bill banning lead from toys": Associated Press, "Bush Signs Bill Banning Lead from Toys," *NBC News*, August 14, 2008, www.nbcnews.com/id/wbna26199580

"After a wave of financial deregulation": Matthew Sherman, "A Short History of Financial Deregulation in the United States," Center for Economic and Policy Research, July 2009, www.cepr.net/documents/publications/dereg-timeline-2009-07.pdf

"investment banks developed an alphabet soup of new and exotic financial products": Liz Moyer, "The Toxic Alphabet Soup

That Almost Took Down Wall Street Is Staging a Comeback," *CNBC*, September 19, 2018.

"In the early 2000s, Wall Street profits made up a record 40 percent of all U.S. corporate profits": Jordan Weissmann, "How Wall Street Devoured Corporate America," *The Atlantic*, March 5, 2013.

"Goldman Sachs, Bear Stearns, Lehman Brothers, and other firms": Jenny Anderson, "Record Profits Elicit Big Bonuses on Wall Street," *The New York Times*, January 12, 2006.

"With thousands getting bonuses" and *"The New York Times noted"*: Anderson, "Record Profits Elicit Big Bonuses."

"Overall, the household sector seems to be in good shape": U.S. Federal Reserve Board, "Remarks by Chairman Alan Greenspan, Understanding Household Debt Obligations, at the Credit Union National Association Governmental Affairs Conference, February 23, 2004," www.federalreserve.gov/boarddocs/speeches/2004/20040223

"Although we certainly cannot rule out home price declines": Testimony of Chairman Alan Greenspan, *The Economic Outlook, Before the Joint Economic Committee, U.S. Congress, June 9, 2005*, U.S. Federal Reserve Board, www.federalreserve.gov/boarddocs/testimony/2005/200506092/default.htm

"I don't see [subprime mortgage market troubles] imposing a serious problem": Reuters, "Treasury's Paulson—Subprime Woes Likely Contained," April 20, 2007, www.reuters.com/article/usa-subprime-paulson/treasurys-paulson-subprime-woes-likely-contained-idUKWBT00686520070420

"former Goldman Sachs CEO Henry Paulson" Goldman Sachs, "Hank Paulson Is Named Chairman and CEO," press release, 1999, www.goldmansachs.com/our-firm/history/moments/1999-paulson-ceo.html

"In terms of looking at housing, most of us believe": "Paulson: Housing 'At or Near Bottom,'" CNNMoney.com, July 2, 2007.

"Paulson's 2005 compensation package": Anderson, "Record Profits Elicit Big Bonuses."

"I'm not an economist, but my hope is" and *"BUSH: 'SOFT LANDING' FOR MARKETS"*: "Bush: 'Soft Landing' for Markets: He Expects Investors to Calm Down and Share His Optimism About the Economy's Soundness," *The Tampa Bay Times*, August 9, 2007.

Tampa Bay Times headline: "Bush: 'Soft Landing' for Markets."

"The worst is likely behind us": Michael M. Phillips and Damian Paletta, "Paulson Sees Credit Crisis Waning," *The Wall Street Journal*, May 7, 2008.

"In September 2008, the collapse of Lehman Brothers triggered an economic crash": Renae Merle, "A Guide to the Financial Crisis—10 years later," *The Washington Post*, September 10, 2018.

"cost taxpayers trillions": Deborah Lucas, "Measuring the Cost of Bailouts," *Annual Review of Financial Economics*, 11 (December 2019): 85–108, doi:10.1146/annurev-financial-110217-022532

"saw nearly nine million people lose their jobs and at least 10 million lose their homes": Colleen Shalby, "The Financial Crisis Hit 10 Years Ago. For Some It Feels Like Yesterday," *Los Angeles Times*, September 15, 2018.

"Thirteen months after the crash, the unemployment rate reached ten percent": Merle, "A Guide to the Financial Crisis."

"with many out of work for half a year or more": *Long-Term Unemployment in the Great Recession, Testimony Before the Joint Economic Committee of Congress, April 29, 2010. Senate Hearing on Long-Term Unemployment: Causes, Consequences, and Solutions*, 111th Cong. (statement of Lawrence Katz, Harvard University).

Thank You for Smoking

"a Surgeon General's study group": Allan Pusey, "July 12, 1957: Surgeon General Links Smoking and Lung Cancer," *ABA Journal* (July 1, 2014).

"the research showing smoking's myriad health risks—including emphysema, pregnancy problems, and addiction": Centers for Disease Control and Prevention (CDC), "Smoking and Tobacco Use—Health Effects," www.cdc.gov/tobacco/index.htm

"Cigarette Smoking Linked to Cancer in High Degree": Harold M. Schmeck Jr., "Cigarette Smoking Linked to Cancer in High Degree; American Society Makes Final Report on Study of 187,783 Men—Industry Disputes Statistical Studies; Smoking Linked to Lung Cancer; A Causative Factor Earlier Findings Checked," *The New York Times*, June 5, 1957.

"Smokers assured in industry study": "Smokers Assured in Industry Study; Report by Tobacco Council Finds No Cigarette Link to Cancer and Heart Disease," *The New York Times*, August 17, 1964.

"People in this country have a right to make up their minds": James C. Bowling, interview by Mike Wallace, *60 Minutes*, CBS, July 18, 1973. Accessed via Truth Tobacco Industry Documents Archive of the University of California, San Francisco, industrydocuments.ucsf.edu/tobacco/docs/#id=nydb0101

"No causal link between smoking and disease has been established": Cristine Russell, "Cigarette Makers Resist Stronger Warning Labels," *The Washington Post*, March 13, 1982.

"CIGARETTES LINKED TO CANCER IN LUNGS": William L. Laurence, "Cigarettes Linked to Cancer in Lungs; Study of 200 Male Sufferers Shows 95.5% Were Heavy Smokers 20 Years," *The New York Times*, February 27, 1949.

"The fact is that there is nothing about smoking, or about the nicotine": Letter to a smoker by Jo Spach, RJR Public Relations Dept., cited in Judge Gladys Kessler, Amended Opinion of the U.S. District Court for the District of Columbia, August 17, 2006, publichealthlawcenter.org/sites/default/files/resources/doj-final-opinion.pdf

"The allegation that smoking cigarettes is addictive is part of a growing and disturbing trend": Hearing of the House Energy and Commerce Committee, Subcommittee on Health and the Environment, 103d Cong. (April 14, 1994). Accessed via *Frontline*, PBS, www.pbs.org/wgbh/pages/frontline/shows/settlement/timelines/april94.html

"Tobacco Chiefs Say Cigarettes Aren't Addictive": Philip J. Hilts, "Tobacco Chiefs Say Cigarettes Aren't Addictive," *The New York Times*, April 15, 1994.

"I believe nicotine is not addictive, yes. . . . And I, too, believe that nicotine is not addictive": Hearing on the Regulation of Tobacco Products, House Energy and Commerce Committee Subcommittee on Health and the Environment, 103d Cong. (April 14, 1994). Accessed via "Tobacco CEO's Statement to Congress 1994 News Clip: 'Nicotine is not addictive,'" University of California San Francisco Academic Senate, senate.ucsf.edu/tobacco-ceo-statement-to-congress

"In fact, a report released six years earlier" Martin Tolchin, "Surgeon General Asserts Smoking Is an Addiction," *The New York Times*, May 17, 1988.

"'Its conclusions reflected the growing'": Tolchin, "Surgeon General Asserts."

"Office workers are routinely exposed to a variety of so-called carcinogens": 103 Cong. Rec. S18425 (August 3, 1993) (statement of Sen. McConnell).

"appears to have been drafted by the Tobacco Institute": Hearing on H.R. 881 (April 19, 1993) (statement of Rep. Emerson). See "1993 04 19 TI Drafted Statements for Lawmakers," contributed by Tom Dreisbach (NPR), Document Cloud, documentcloud

.org/documents/6007509-1993-04-19-TI-Drafted-Statements-for-Lawmakers.html#document/p11/a501681

"Time for a quick reality check": Jason Silverstein, "Mike Pence Said Smoking 'Doesn't Kill' and Faced Criticism for His Response to HIV. Now He's Leading the Coronavirus Response," CBSNews.com, February 29, 2020.

"nearly half a million Americans die prematurely": CDC, "Smoking and Tobacco Use, Data and Statistics."

Case Study: Climate Change

"Wake up, America. With all the hysteria": 108 Cong. Rec., S. 10012 (July 28, 2003), www.govinfo.gov/content/pkg/CREC-2003-07-28/html/CREC-2003-07-28-pt1-PgS10012.htm

"Inhofe was mocked for bringing a snowball into Senate chambers": Philip Bump, "Jim Inhofe's Snowball Has Disproven Climate Change Once and for All," *The Washington Post*, February 26, 2015.

"STUDY FINDS WARMING TREND THAT COULD RAISE SEA LEVELS": Walter Sullivan, "Study Finds Warming Trend That Could Raise Sea Levels," *The New York Times*, August 22, 1981.

"the front page of the New York Times *trumpeted a study"*: Sullivan, "Study Finds Warming Trend."

"committed themselves to action": Nathaniel Rich, "Losing Earth: The Decade We Almost Stopped Climate Change," *The New York Times*, August 1, 2018.

"as it became clear that major changes would be needed": Philip Shabecoff, "Global Warming Has Begun, Expert Tells Senate; Sharp Cut in Burning of Fossil Fuels Is Urged to Battle Shift in Climate," *The New York Times*, June 24, 1988.

"campaigned to become 'the environmental president'": "Bush vs. Clinton: What Is an Environmental President," *Los Angeles Times*, September 27, 1992.

"His chief of staff, John Sununu": Rich, "Losing Earth."

"I don't want anyone in this administration without a scientific background": Rich, "Losing Earth."

"Global Warming Has Begun, Expert Tells Senate": Shabecoff, "Global Warming Has Begun."

"previously shown that climate change was real": Climate Files, "1982 Memo to Exxon Management About CO2 Greenhouse Effect," www.climatefiles.com/exxonmobil/1982-memo-to-exxon-management-about-co2-greenhouse-effect

"In spite of the rush by some participants": Climate Files, "1989 Presentation to Exxon Board of Directors on Greenhouse Gas Effects," www.climatefiles.com/exxonmobil/1989-presentation-exxon-board-directors-greenhouse-gas-effects/

"That same year": Rich, "Losing Earth."

"'Throughout the 1990s'": Bill McKibben, "Climate of Denial," *Mother Jones*, May–June 2005.

"In 1992 the GCC distributed": Climate Files, "1992 Western Fuels Association *The Greening of Planet Earth*," www.climatefiles.com/trade-group/1992-western-fuels-greening-planet-earth

"None of the documentary's participants": Climate Files, "1992 Western Fuels Association."

"You should see a real greening of the desert": "*The Greening of Planet Earth* (transcript)," contributed by Casey (Climate Investigations Center) Document Cloud, documentcloud.org/documents/4776001-The-Greening-of-Planet-Earth-Transcript#document/p7/a447937

"In terms of plant growth": "*The Greening of Planet Earth* (transcript)."

"On the eve of the 1997 Kyoto Protocol": United Nations Climate Change, "What Is the Kyoto Protocol?" https://unfccc .int/kyoto_protocol#:~:text=In%20short%2C%20the%20 Kyoto%20Protocol,accordance%20with%20agreed%20 individual%20targets

"(estimated cost: $31,)": Geoffrey Supran and Naomi Oreskes, "What Exxon Mobil Didn't Say About Climate Change," *The New York Times*, August 22, 2017.

"Let's face it; The science of climate change is too uncertain": Supran and Oreskes, "What Exxon Mobil Didn't Say."

"Although President Bill Clinton signed the Kyoto treaty in 1998": Environmental Defense Fund, "President Clinton Signs Climate Treaty," November 12, 1998, www.edf.org/news /president-clinton-signs-climate-treaty

"the Senate refused to ratify it": Helen Dewar and Kevin Sullivan, "Senate Republicans Call Kyoto Pact Dead," *The Washington Post*, December 11, 1997.

"President George W. Bush withdrew from the pact in 2001": Julian Border, "Bush Kills Global Warming Treaty," *The Guardian*, March 29, 2001.

"Global warming is a myth": Andrew Kaczynski, "Smoking Doesn't Kill and Other Great Old Op-Eds from Mike Pence," *Buzzfeed News*, March 31, 2015.

"The Earth will be able to support enormously more people": Andrew Goldman, "The Billionaire Party," *New York Magazine*, July 23, 2010.

"I have a theory about global warming and why people think it's real": Jocelyn Fong and Shauna Theel, "Rush Limbaugh: Climate Change Misinformer of the Year," *Media Matters*, December 19, 2011.

"In the beautiful Midwest, windchill temperatures": Joe Tacopina, "Trump Mocks Global Warming in Tweet amid Midwest Chill," *The New York Post*, January 28, 2019.

2: The Free Market Knows Best

"We are close to the line where government expansion": Lawrence B. Glickman, *Free Enterprise: An American History* (New Haven, CT: Yale University Press, 2019), 9.

"Left to their own devices, it is alleged, businessmen": Bill Goldstein, "Word for Word/'When Greenspan Shrugged': When Greed Was a Virtue and Regulation the Enemy," *The New York Times*, July 21, 2002.

"'a mixed economy'": Dave Anderson, "President Trump Is Not a Capitalist," *The Hill*, March 4, 2019.

"During the Great Depression, however, as government expanded": U.S. Library of Congress, "U.S. History Primary Source Timeline: President Franklin Delano Roosevelt and the New Deal," www.loc.gov/classroom-materials/united-states -history-primary-source-timeline/great-depression-and -world-war-ii-1929-1945/franklin-delano-roosevelt-and-the -new-deal/

"The free market, said Ogden Mills": Glickman, *Free Enterprise*, 3.

"If you're still paying for cable TV": Richard Greenfield, "How the Cable Industry Became a Monopoly," *Fortune*, May 19, 2015.

"Income and inheritance taxes, which are in effect confiscatory": "Confiscation of Wealth," *Chicago Daily Tribune*, January 17, 1932.

"It would result in further and unnecessary intrusion": Hearings on Income, Inheritance, and Gift Taxation, House Committee on Ways and Means, 73d Cong. (March 21–24, 26–30, 1934) (statement by James L. Donnelly, Executive Vice President, Illinois Manufacturers' Association).

"It is important to public health, therefore": Drug Industry Act of 1962: Hearings before House Committee on Interstate and Foreign Commerce, 87th Cong. (June 19, 1962) (statement of Eugene N. Beesley, President, Eli Lilly).

"Many companies have cut back drastically": Naegele testimony, House Committee on Agriculture, March 8, 1971.

"High Pesticide Levels Seen in U.S. Food": Marian Burros, "High Pesticide Levels Seen in U.S. Food," *The New York Times*, February 19, 1999.

"In the first three decades of the 20th century, over 68, coal miners": U.S. Department of Labor, Mine Safety and Health Administration, "Coal Fatalities, 1900–2020," https://arlweb.msha.gov/stats/centurystats/coalstats.asp

"In recent years the accident record in the bituminous coal industry": Farrington testimony, Senate Subcommittee on Mines and Mining, June 19, 1947.

"The coal industry accepts its responsibilities": Bailey testimony, House Subcommittee on Labor Standards, June 7, 1977.

"We feel that in a free competitive economy": Dennis A. Deslippe, *Rights Not Roses: Unions and the Rise of Working Class Feminism, 1945–1980* (Urbana-Champaign: University of Illinois Press, 1999), 51.

"The act will tend to cause labor unrest": Becker testimony, House Committee Hearing, Equal Pay Act, March 26, 1963.

"We cannot ignore the variables inherent": Edwards testimony, House Committee Hearing, Equal Pay Act, March 26, 1963.

"But the debate over the 1968 Occupational Health and Safety Act": U.S. Department of Labor, OSH Act of 1970, www.osha.gov/laws-regs/oshact/completeoshact

"In striving to improve safety and healthful conditions in the workplace": Logan testimony, Senate Subcommittee on Labor and Public Welfare, June 12, 1968.

"Prior to the passage of this legislation, certain special-interest groups": Berman testimony, the Select Subcommittee on Labor of the House Committee on Education and Labor, September 14, 1972.

"Employers do not deliberately allow work conditions": Chamber of Commerce, "OSHA—Crying Need for Fair Play," Chamber of Commerce newsletter, June 1973.

"In 1970, the year it was passed": Michaels and Barab, "The Occupational Safety and Health Administration at 50."

"This approach assumes that all consumers want the same thing": Kraus testimony, Legislation and Military Operations Subcommittee of the House Government Operations Committee, October 9, 1973.

"To the extent that [this legislation] seeks to make varying warranties": *Consumer Products Guaranty Act of 1970: Hearings Before the Committee on Commerce Consumer Subcommittee*, 91st Cong., 2d Sess. (January 22, 1970) (statement of Aaron Yohalem, General Electric Consumer Issues Subcommittee).

"took billions of dollars in government funds": Brett Snavely, "Taxpayers Auto Bailout Loss $9.3B," *Detroit Free Press*, December 30, 2014.

"From a commercial standpoint in a competitive marketplace": Environmental Working Group, "Blind Spot: The Big Three's Attack on the Global Warming Treaty" [Donner testimony, Subcommittee on Executive Reorganization of the Senate Committee on Government Operations, July 13, 1965].

"HENRY FORD SEES ECONOMIC HAZARD IN CURB ON AUTOS": Walter Rugaber, "Henry Ford Sees Economic Hazard in Curb on Autos; Calls on Congress to Avoid 'Irrational' Safety Steps Assails Industry Critics," *The New York Times*, April 16, 1966.

"If we sell too many big cars, we'll have to stop building them":

Terry testimony on the Energy Policy and Conservation Act, September 14, 1976.

"[The Medicare bill would] set up a health care program": Hearings Before the Committee on Finance, U.S. Senate, 89th Cong., 1st Sess. on H. R. 6675 (1965), 421 (statement by Raymond E. King, Jr., National Association of Life Underwriters).

"the 1985 measure we now know as COBRA": U.S. Congress, Consolidated Omnibus Budget Reconciliation Act of 1985, congress.gov/bill/99th-congress/house-bill/3128

"The problem of lack of health insurance for the unemployed": Ozga testimony, Senate Finance Committee, April 21, 1983.

"Forcing free market plans to compete with these government-run programs": Letter to the White House from Sens. Mitch McConnell, Orrin Hatch, Charles Grassley, Mike Enzi, and Judd Gregg, June 6, 2009.

"Small firms who have hired persons with disabilities": Sally Douglas, "Should the Senate Approve the Americans with Disabilities Act of 1989? CON," *The Congressional Digest*, December 1, 1989.

"The push to get the U.S.": U.S. Department of Labor, Family and Medical Leave Act of 1993, www.dol.gov/agencies/whd/laws-and-regulations/laws/fmla

"Including the previous president who vetoed it": Stephen A. Holmes, "House Backs Bush Veto of Family Leave Bill," *The New York Times*, July 26, 1990.

"We must also recognize that mandated benefits": From Bush's veto message, June 29, 1990, accessed on the website of Congressional Quarterly.

"ENDA should be opposed by anyone who believes": Peter Sprigg, "Employment Non-Discrimination Act Threatens Free Markets," CNN, March 22, 2013.

"The subprime mortgage market, which makes funds available":

Jeffrey Gunther, "Should CRA Stand for 'Community Redundancy Act?'" *Regulation*, 2, no. 3 (November 8, 2).

"If you compare what the card industry looked like 20 years ago": Thomas Brown, "Chris Dodd's Credit Card Bill Will Help Consumers? Don't Count on It," BankStocks.com, May 1, 2009.

"Of course, the subprime mortgage market": Kristopher Gerardi, Adam Hale Shapiro, and Paul S. Willen, "Subprime Outcomes: Risky Mortgages, Homeownership Experiences, and Foreclosures" (working paper, Federal Reserve Bank of Boston, May 4, 2008).

"saved consumers over $16 billion": Consumer Financial Protection Bureau, "CFPB Finds CARD Act Helped Consumers Avoid Over $16 Billion in Gotcha Credit Card Fees," press release, December 3, 2015.

"Most of the programs in the plan are redistribution": Brian Darling, "Biden Build Back Better Plan Will Kill Economic Growth," *The Washington Times*, September 30, 2021.

"The Biden model is so heavily taxing and regulating": Larry Kudlow, "Kudlow: Free Enterprise Drives the American Economic Machine," *Fox Business*, July 20, 2021.

"Quite simply, the plan is a rejection of the American system": David Ditch et al., "President Biden's Tax-and-Spend Plan Expands Federal Power, Not Jobs," Heritage Foundation, May 11, 2021.

Case Study: Civil Rights: "A Step Toward the Destruction of Free Enterprise"

"the 1941 Fair Employment Practices Commission": U.S. National Archives, "Prohibition of Discrimination in the Defense Industry," Executive Order 8802, June 25, 1941, www.archives.gov/milestone-documents/executive-order-8802

"Another nail in the coffin": Timothy N. Thurber, *Republicans and Race, The GOP's Frayed Relationship with African Americans, 1945–1974* (Lawrence: University of Kansas Press, 2013).

"[The FEPC is] a step toward the destruction": Glickman, *Free Enterprise.*

"Not until 1964 did Congress": U.S. Equal Employment Opportunity Commission, Title VII of the Civil Rights Act of 1964, www.eeoc.gov/statutes/title-vii-civil-rights-act-1964

"Our organization will carry on": Chris Myers Asch, *The Senator and the Sharecropper: The Freedom Struggles of James O. Eastland and Fannie Lou Hamer* (Chapel Hill: University of North Carolina Press, 2008).

"[Free enterprise] includes not only freedom from": Glickman, *Free Enterprise*, 207.

"This lunch counter was his property": James J. Kilpatrick, *The Southern Case for School Segregation* (New York: Crowell-Collier, 1962).

"I am having nothing to do with enforcing a law": George Wallace, "The Civil Rights Movement: Fraud, Sham and Hoax," *American Experience*, PBS, July 4, 1964.

"[The bill authorizes] such vast governmental control": Jason Morgan Ward, *Defending White Democracy* (Chapel Hill: University of North Carolina Press, 2011).

"We have a divine right to discriminate": Kevin M. Kruse, *White Flight: Atlanta and the Making of Modern Conservatism* (Princeton, NJ: Princeton University Press, 2005).

"Maddox led a march for 'freedom'": "Lester Maddox Leads Segregation Marchers," *Hendersonville Times-News*, April 26, 1965.

"Maddox said it portended": "Atlanta Restaurant Closes, But Owner Continues to Fight," *Tuscaloosa News*, August 14, 1964.

"He reopened it as a museum,": Glickman, *Free Enterprise*, 206.

"Private racism is not a legal, but a moral issue": Ayn Rand, "The Virtue of Selfishness," Ayn Rand Institute, September 1963, aynrand.org/novels/the-virtue-of-selfishness/

"Is there any difference in principle": Milton Friedman, "Economic and Political Freedom," in *The Capitalist Reader*, ed. Lawrence S. Stepelevich (Eugene, OR: Wipf and Stock, 2019).

"He was perhaps the most influential": Greg Ip and Mark Whitehouse, "How Milton Friedman Changed Economics, Policy, and Markets," *The Wall Street Journal*, November 17, 2006.

"persistent racial disparities in employment and wages": Eileen Patten, "Racial, Gender Wage Gaps Persist in U.S. Despite Some Progress," Pew Research Center, July 1, 2016.

"chronic under-funding of federal efforts to root out on-the-job discrimination": Maryam Jameel, "More and More Workplace Discrimination Cases Are Being Closed Before They're Even Investigated," *Vox*, June 14, 2019.

"The start of the evil can be pinpointed": Murray Rothbard, "The Great Thomas and Hill Show: Stopping the Monstrous Regiment," LewRockwell.com.

"The Civil Rights Act of 1964 gave the federal government unprecedented power": Alex Seitz-Wald, "Ron Paul Suggests We'd Be 'Better Off' Without the Civil Rights Act," ThinkProgress, May 14, 2011.

"A free society will abide unofficial, private discrimination": Rand Paul, "Letter to the Editor," *Bowling Green Daily News*, May 30, 2002.

"I think it's a bad business decision to exclude anybody": Glenn Kessler, "Rand Paul's Rewriting of His Own Remarks on the Civil Rights Act," *The Washington Post*, April 11, 2013.

"I would not go to that Woolworth's": Kessler, "Rand Paul's Rewriting of His Own Remarks."

"Libertarians should not only oppose Title II": Jeffrey Miron,

"What Matters Are Consequences, Not Context," *Cato Unbound: A Journal of Ideas*, June 23, 2010.

Facebook's "Big Tobacco Moment"

"'*Facebook and Big Tech,*'": Cecilia Kang, "Lawmakers See a Path to Rein in Big Tech, But It Isn't Smooth," *The New York Times*, October 9, 2021.

"*Richard Blumenthal of Connecticut, who led a successful suit*": Matthew Daly, "State Files $1 Billion Lawsuit Against 10 Tobacco Companies," *The Hartford Courant*, July 19, 1996.

"*Facebook has pioneered efforts to reach an ever-younger audience*": Ezra Kaplan and Jo Ling Kent, "Documents Reveal Facebook Targeted Children as Young as Six for Consumer Base," NBCNews.com, October 29, 2021.

"*internal Facebook research on Instagram use*": Georgia Wells, Jeff Horwitz, and Deepa Seetharaman, "Facebook Knows Instagram Is Toxic for Teen Girls, Company Documents Show," *The Wall Street Journal*, September 14, 2021.

"*The research that we've seen is that using social apps*": Wells, Horwitz, Seetharaman, "Facebook Knows Instagram Is Toxic."

"*testimony by whistleblower Frances Haugen*": Reed Albergotti, "Frances Haugen Took Thousands of Facebook Documents: This Is How She Did It," *The Washington Post*, October 26, 2021.

"*I don't know any tech company that sets out to build*": Tim Baysinger, "Mark Zuckerberg Defends Facebook Following Whistleblower Senate Testimony: 'Most of the Claims Don't Make Any Sense'," Yahoo News, October 5, 2021.

3: It's Not Our Fault, It's Your Fault

"*Legislation cannot remedy the evils*": Graebner, *Coal-Mining Safety*, 113.

"*[Do] we really want to subsidize*": "Rick Santelli and 'The Rant of the Year'" (originally aired CNBC February 24, 2006), YouTube, youtube.com/watch?v=bEZB4taSEoA&t=4s

"*a long history of devastating accidents*": "U.S. Mine Disasters Fast Facts," CNN.com, March 1, 2021.

"*Such accidents are little short of deliberate suicide*": Graebner, *Coal-Mining Safety*, 74.

"*[The bill will] not strike at the fundamental cause*": Farrington testimony, Senate Subcommittee on Mines and Mining, June 19, 1947.

"*Training and education in themselves are no panacea*": Bailey testimony, House Subcommittee on Labor Standards, June 7, 1977.

"*2010 disaster at Massey Energy's Upper Big Branch Mine*": "A Timeline of Events in Upper Big Branch Disaster," *Associated Press*, October 1, 2015.

"*Either something went wrong*": Ken Ward Jr., "Massey Board Standing by Blankenship," *West Virginia Gazette Mail*, April 22, 2010.

"'*a badge of honor*'": Jocelyn King, "Senate Candidate and Former Coal CEO Don Blankenship Blames MSHA, Considers Conviction a 'Badge of Honor' in West Virginia," *The Intelligencer* and *Wheeling News Register*, March 16, 2018.

"*The only tendency toward illness comes to men*": Factory Investigating Commission, Preliminary Report, III, 675.

"*The essential thing necessary to safely*": David Rosner and Gerald E. Markowitz, *Dying for Work: Workers' Safety and Health in 20th Century America* (Bloomington: Indiana University Press, 1987), 130.

"The only seemingly feasible means": David Rosner and Gerald E. Markowitz, *Deceit and Denial: The Deadly Politics of Industrial Pollution* (Berkeley: University of California Press, 2013), 95.

"I have yet to see a woman": Miller testimony, House hearing on Equal Pay Act, March 26, 1963.

"You can't really blame the U.S. Chamber of Commerce": "Ladies' Day in the Senate," *The Wall Street Journal*, August 15, 1962.

"Roads, laws and cars are inanimate": Ralph Nader, *Unsafe at Any Speed*, 25th anniversary ed. (New York: Knightsbridge Publishing: 1991), 232.

"sales hit a record high": Clare M. Reckert, "Surge in U.S. Rubber's Profits Brightens Meeting," *The New York Times*, April 22, 1964.

"'unsafe acts,' not 'unsafe conditions'": U.S. House Committee on Education and Labor, H.R. Rep. No. 1720, 90th Cong., 2d Sess. (July 16, 1968).

"The really important progress in occupational safety": Charles Noble, *Liberalism at Work: The Rise and Fall of OSHA* (Philadelphia, PA: Temple University Press, 1986), 84.

"We find that 80 to 90 percent of the injuries": Queener testimony, House Select Subcommittee on Labor, February 29, 1968.

"The vast majority of accidents result from human": "Life or Death for Your Business?" *Nation's Business*, April 1968, in U.S. Senate, *Hearings Before the Subcommittee on Labor of the Committee on Labor and Public Welfare*, 90th Cong., 2d Sess. on S. 2864, (February 15, June 12, 19, 24, 28, and July 2, 1968), 796.

"[We don't] believe safety can be achieved": Naumann testimony, Senate Subcommittee on Labor and Public Welfare, June 12, 1968.

"speeding laws do indeed help stop speeding": Lee S. Friedman,

Donald Hedeker, and Elihu D. Richter, "Long-Term Effects of Repealing the National Maximum Speed Limit in the United States," *American Journal of Public Health*, 99, no. 9 (September 2009): 1626–1631.

"The [cotton dust] problem is grossly exaggerated": Margo Hornblower, "Brown-Lung Protection Urged," *The Washington Post*, April 22, 1977.

"a compound in many aerosol products that damaged the ozone layer": U.S. Environmental Protection Agency, "Basic Ozone Layer Science," www.epa.gov/ozone-layer-protection/basic-ozone-layer-science

"People who don't stand out in the sun": "Editorial: Through Rose-Colored Sunglasses," *The New York Times*, May 31, 1987.

"Every individual chooses if and how": Lori Dorfman, Lawrence Wallack, and Katie Woodruff, "More Than a Message: Framing Public Health Advocacy to Change Corporate Practices," *Health Education & Behavior*, 32, no. 3 (June 2005): 331.

"I wouldn't say we're part of the [obesity] problem": David Barboza, "The Media Business: Advertising; A Warning in Expanding Waistlines," *The New York Times*, July 10, 2003.

"Our position is that the individual who is concerned": "Restaurants Urged to Give Customers Nutrition Information," *Food Processing: The Magazine of the Food Industry*, February 16, 2005.

"The decision to smoke or not": Jack Germond and Jules Witcover, "There's Smoke—and Fire," *The Chicago Tribune*, January 9, 1978.

"When you've got on the label": Rudolph A. Pyatt Jr. and Sari Horwitz, "Tobacco Firms Step Up Efforts to Diversify," *The Washington Post*, October 6, 1985.

"When Purdue Pharma introduced": Shraddha Chakradhar and Casey Ross, "The History of OxyContin, Told Through Unsealed Purdue Documents," *Stat News*, December 3, 2019.

"States, cities and counties sued": Opioid Settlement Tracker, "States' Opioid Settlement Statuses," opioidsettlementtracker. com

"We have to hammer": Andrew Joseph, "'A Blizzard of Prescriptions': Documents Reveal New Details About Purdue's Marketing of OxyContin," *Stat News*, January 15, 2019.

"We intend to stay the course" and *"It's not addiction, it's abuse"*: "Mass AGO Pre-Hearing Memo and Exhibits," *Commonwealth of Massachusetts lawsuit v. Purdue Pharma L.P. et al.*, Suffolk County Superior Court, C.A. No. 1884-cv-01808 (BLS2), www.documentcloud.org/documents/5684879-Mass -AGO-Pre-Hearing-Memo-and-Exhibits.html

"An internal note from then-Purdue CEO Craig Landau": Joseph, "'A Blizzard of Prescriptions.'"

"facing 2,900 lawsuits, Purdue filed for bankruptcy": Jan Hoffman and Mary Williams Walsh, "Purdue Pharma, Maker of OxyContin, Files for Bankruptcy," *The New York Times*, September 15, 2019.

"Former head of OxyContin maker": "Former Head of OxyContin Maker Purdue Pharma Denies Blame for Opioid Crisis," CBS News, August 18, 2021.

"Two years later, a federal settlement": Jan Hoffman, "Purdue Pharma Is Dissolved and Sacklers Pay $4.5 Billion to Settle Opioid Claims," *The New York Times*, September 1, 2021.

"Many plaintiffs attacked the judgment": Jan Hoffman and Mary Williams Walsh, "Judge Clears Purdue Pharma's Restructuring Plan for Vote by Thousands of Claimants," *The New York Times*, May 26, 2021.

"thanks largely to risky lending practices": Erin Coghlan, Lisa McCorkell, and Sara Hinkley, *What Really Caused the Great Recession* (Berkeley, CA: Institute for Research on Labor and Employment, 2018).

"The government is promoting bad behavior": "Rick Santelli and 'The Rant of the Year.'"

"It wasn't the Bush administration": David M. Abromowitz, "Sen. Kyl Tries to Blame Economic Mess on Democrats, 'Minorities,' 'the Poor,' and 'the Young,'" *HuffPost*, March 26, 2008.

"The Mother of All Bailouts has many fathers": Michelle Malkin, "Illegal Loans," *National Review Online*, September 24, 2008.

"Americans own almost 400 million guns": Christopher Ingraham, "There Are More Guns Than People in the United States, According to a New Study of Global Firearm Ownership," *The Washington Post*, June 19, 2018.

"researchers say they are at least part of the reason": Zack Beauchamp, "America Doesn't Have More Crime Than Other Rich Countries. It Just Has More Guns," *Vox*, February 15, 2018.

"Most American gun owners support": Mike Lillis, "Poll: 92 Percent of Gun Owners Support Universal Background Checks," *The Hill*, July 3, 2014.

"blocked promising reforms": Brian Schwartz, "NRA Spent $1.6 Million Lobbying Against Background Check Expansion Laws in Months Leading Up to Latest Mass Shootings," CNBC.com, August 5, 2019.

"There are two wildly different gun cultures": Frank Miniter, "America Has Two Gun Cultures: Don't Blame Law-Abiding Gun Owners for Murders," FoxNews.com, February 21, 2018.

"We don't go around shooting people": Lexington [David Rennie], "Why the NRA Keeps Talking About Mental Illness, Rather Than Guns," *The Economist*, March 13, 2013.

"We have no national database of these lunatics": Wayne LaPierre, *Meet the Press*, NBC News, December 23, 2012.

"research shows that having access to a gun": Kaitlin Sullivan, "Mental Illness Isn't a Major Risk Factor for Gun Violence, but Here's What Is," NBCNews.com, August 6, 2019.

"LaPierre nevertheless opposes": Lexington, "Why the NRA Keeps Talking About Mental Illness."

Case Study: Tort Reform

"In the 1980s, industry began pushing 'tort reform'": U.S. Chamber of Commerce Institute for Legal Reform, "History of Tort Reform," instituteforlegalreform.com/history-of-tort-reform/

"In 1992, 79-year-old Stella Liebeck": Andrea Gerlin, "How a Jury Decided That a Coffee Spill Is Worth $2.9 Million," *The Wall Street Journal*, September 1, 1994.

"ABC News has called the case": Lauren Pearle, "I'm Being Sued for WHAT?" ABCNews.com, May 2, 2007.

"In fact, McDonald's had a policy": Gerlin, "How a Jury Decided."

"She sued only after first": Gerlin, "How a Jury Decided."

"A lady goes to a fast-food restaurant": "Scalded by Coffee, Then News Media," Retro Report, *The New York Times*, October 21, 2013 (see 9:03 mark in video).

"Every action we take in life carries with it": Citizens Against Legal Abuse (CALA) [author query]

"First-person accounts by sundry women": Gerlin, "How a Jury Decided."

"If the plaintiff was injured and damaged": Hyungjin Kim and Jungwoo Kim, esq., "Case: The Stella Liebeck Trial, Known as the McDonald's Hot Coffee," *The Global Business Law*, 2nd. ed. (Goyang, Gyeonggi, Korea: Quseum, 2020).

"Mrs. Liebeck's age": Gerlin, "How a Jury Decided."

"reduced by a judge": "Judge Cuts Award in Scalding Coffee Suit to $640," *Los Angeles Times*, September 15, 1994.

"Jay Leno made Liebeck into the butt": "Scalded by Coffee" (see 8:22 mark in video).

"Talk radio went crazy": "Scalded by Coffee" (see 8:30 mark in video).

"referenced on Seinfeld": "Scalded by Coffee" (see 9:50 mark in video).

"Plasma gettin' bigger": "Scalded by Coffee" (see 10:28 mark in video).

"Anyone who's ever bought take-out beverages": "Editorial: Can't We Be Responsible for Drinking a Cup of Coffee," *Greensboro News and Record*, May 6, 1995.

"What do Stella Liebeck, Alecia Wallace": Zay N. Smith, "Techies Find Slick Use for Hog Waste," *Chicago Sun Times*, August 6, 1995.

"Newt Gingrich and congressional Republicans": Dan Balz, "GOP 'Contract' Pledges 10 Tough Acts to Follow," *The Washington Post*, November 20, 1994.

"Texas passed seven different major bills": George Lardner Jr., "'Tort Reform': Mixed Results," *The Washington Post*, February 10, 2.

"numerous other states passed similar packages": U.S. Chamber of Commerce Institute for Legal Reform, "History of Tort Reform."

"major theme of Gov. George W. Bush's successful run": Lardner, "'Tort Reform.'"

"Stella Liebeck died in 2004": "Scalded by Coffee" (see 11:32 mark in video).

"'I was not in it for the money,'": "Scalded by Coffee" (see 3:16 mark in video).

4: It's a Job Killer

"Never in the history of the world has any measure": Taber's speech following House vote on the Social Security Act, April 19, 1935.

"Increasing worker pay doesn't result in cost hikes or job losses": Annie Lowrey, "The Counterintuitive Workings of the Minimum Wage," *The Atlantic*, January 29, 2021; Annie Fadely, "The Congressional Budget Office Says Raising the Minimum Wage to $15 Will Kill Jobs. That's Not the Whole Truth—Here's Why," *Insider*, February 13, 2021; Ben Zipperer, "Gradually Raising the Minimum Wage to $15 Would Be Good for Workers, Good for Businesses, and Good for the Economy," *Economic Policy Institute*, February 7, 2019.

"Paid family leave and sick day laws": Trish Stroman et al., "Why Paid Family Leave Is Good Business," Boston Consulting Group, February 7, 2017, https://media-publications.bcg.com/BCG-Why-Paid-Family-Leave-Is-Good-Business-Feb-2017.pdf

"a period when corporations and the wealthy paid a far higher tax rate,": The Tax Foundation, "Historical Corporate Top Tax Rate and Bracket, 1909–2014," taxfoundation.org/historical-corporate-tax-rates-brackets/

"when profits were shared far more equally,": Chad Stone et al., "A Guide to Statistics on Historical Trends in Income Inequality," Center on Budget and Policy Priorities, January 13, 2020.

"and when worker protections were stronger than today": Elizabeth Tandy Shermer, "The Right to Work Really Means the Right to Work for Less," *The Washington Post*, April 24, 2018.

"there's little evidence that the states and cities that have raised their minimum wage to $15 an hour": Sylvia Allegretto et al., "The New Wave of Local Minimum Wage Policies: Evidence from Six Cities," University of California, Berkeley, Center on Wage and Employment Dynamics, September 6, 2018.

"The 1911 New York Triangle Shirtwaist Factory fire": "Triangle Shirtwaist Fire Kills 146 in New York City," History.com

"[Fire code rules will lead to] the wiping out of industry": Harold Meyerson, "The Mind-Set That Survived the Triangle Shirt-waist Fire," *The Washington Post*, March 22, 2011.

"The Real Estate Board of New York is informed": George W. Olvany, "The Fire Hazard in Big Buildings," *The New York Times*, May 3, 1914.

"A state commission didn't find": "Seeks to Simplify Building Inspection," *The New York Times*, July 27, 1914.

"lifting more people out of poverty": Kathleen Romig, "Social Security Lifts More Americans Above Poverty Than Any Other Program," Center on Budget and Policy Priorities, February 20, 2020.

"Polls consistently show overwhelming public support": Lorie Konish, "Preventing Social Security Benefit Cuts Is a Top Priority for Americans in 2020 Election, Survey Finds," CNBC.com, August 19, 2020.

"[The Social Security bill would] discourage employment": Jude Blanchette, "Opponents of the Crown Jewel: Is Social Security the Most Successful Government Program in History?" Foundation for Economic Education, September 1, 2015.

"Do not forget this: Such an excessive tax": Alf Landon, "'I Will Not Promise the Moon': Alf Landon Opposes the Social Security Act, 1936," History Matters: The U.S. Survey Course on the Web, historymatters.gmu.edu/d/8128

"Employers pay men, not machines": Hearings on Unemployment Insurance, House Committee on Ways and Means, 73d Cong. (March 21–24, 26–30, 1934) (statement of John C. Gall, National Association of Manufacturers).

"It will hasten mechanization of all processes": "Insurance Plan Called Ruinous," *Associated Press*, March 31, 1934.

"We have had several young men start out": Miller testimony, House hearing on Equal Pay Act, March 26, 1963.

"I know that there are variables": Edwards testimony, House hearing on Equal Pay Act, March 26, 1963.

"[Consider] the possible impact of this bill": Olverson testimony, House hearing on Equal Pay Act, March 27, 1963.

"Under the guise of civil rights for the disabled": Susan Mandel, "Disabling the GOP," *National Review*, June 11, 1990.

"[The bill] will seriously affect employment": Ruth DeForest Lamb and Royal S. Copeland, *American Chamber of Horrors* (New York: Grosset & Dunlap, 1936), 292–293.

"We would strenuously object to any bill": Otto testimony, hearing of the House Committee on Public Works, June 11, 12 and 16, 1947.

"Entire industries could fold": Joseph P. Glas, "Protecting the Ozone Layer: A Perspective from Industry," in *Technology and Environment*, eds. Jesse H. Ausubel and Hedy E. Sladovitch (Washington, DC: National Academy Press, 1989), 137–155.

"The effects include serious long-term losses": "Women's Suffrage and Other Visions of Right-Wing Apocalypse," *The New Republic*, December 20, 2009.

"This study leaves little doubt that a minimum": Robert Hahn and Wilbur Steger, *An Analysis of Jobs at Risk and Job Losses from the Proposed Clean Air Act Amendments* (Pittsburgh, PA: CONSAD Research Corporation, 1990).

"In fact, a 2011 study": U.S. Environmental Protection Agency, "Benefits and Costs of the Clean Air Act, 1990–2020, the Second Prospective Study," www.epa.gov/clean-air-act-overview/benefits-and-costs-clean-air-act-1990-2020-second-prospective-study

"[T]his bill could prevent continued production": "Women's Suffrage and Other Visions of Right-Wing Apocalypse."

"[It would not be possible] to achieve the control levels": *Hearings Before the Senate Subcommittee on Air and Water Pollution of Senate Committee on Public Works*, 91st Cong., 2d. Sess. (statement of ---, American Automobile Manufacturers Association).

"With the Environmental Protection Agency": James Mateja, "Fuel Economy Law May Force Car Rationing, Detroit Warns," *The Chicago Tribune*, September 14, 1976.

"The whole CAFE scheme is, in terms of public policy, ridiculous": John H. Cushman Jr., "Tougher Fuel Economy Rules Planned, in Shift from Reagan," *The New York Times*, April 15, 1989.

"[Family leave laws are] the greatest threats": Ronald D. Elving, *Conflict and Compromise: How Congress Makes the Law* (New York: Touchstone, 1995), 91.

"It is a job killer": Patrick B. McGuigan, "Istook: Family Leave, Economics, Trade," *The Daily Oklahoman*, October 25, 1992.

"The real world impact of this well-intentioned legislation": Family & Medical Leave Act—Conference Report, *Congressional Record* 1059 (Washington, DC: U.S. Government Printing Office, 1992).

"[The Democratic Party] don't get that the ability" and *"[T]here is nothing pro-family"*: 103 Cong. Rec. H1993 (February 3, 1993) (statement of Mr. DeLay), www.govinfo.gov/content/pkg/GPO-CRECB-1993-pt2/pdf/GPO-CRECB-1993-pt2-4-2.pdf

"2 Department of Labor survey": Jane Waldfogel, "Family and Medical Leave: Evidence from the 2 Surveys," *Monthly Labor Review*, 124, no. 9 (September 1, 2001): 17–23.

"[California] can follow the programs of Germany": Mark Sappenfield, "Next Test for California: Fixing the Business Climate," *The Christian Science Monitor*, April 15, 2004.

"I hope this is a lesson for the next Republican": "State Senate OKs Paid Leave to Care for Others", *Tri-Valley Herald*, June 11, 2002.

"California employers surveyed in 2011": Niesha Lofing, "Study: California's Paid Family Leave Law Hasn't Been a 'Job Killer,'" *The Sacramento Bee*, January 12, 2011.

"President Clinton's 1993 budget bill, which increased corporate taxes": Eric Pianin and David S. Hilzenrath, "Senate Passes Clinton Budget Bill 51–50 After Kerrey Reluctantly Casts 'Yes' Vote," *The Washington Post*, August 7, 1993.

"These new taxes will stifle economic growth": U.S. House of Representatives, *Concurrent Resolution on the Budget, Fiscal Year 1994*, 103 Cong. Rec. H1454 (March 18, 1993).

"Clearly, this is a job-killer in the short-run": Rep. Dick Armey, "Party Representatives Disagree on Deficit-Reduction," CNN, August 2, 1993.

"We're going to find out": GOP News Conference, August 3, 1993, c-spanvideo.org/program/47517-1

"At least 22 million jobs": Center for American Progress, "Power of Progressive Economics: The Clinton Years," October 28, 2011, www.americanprogress.org/article/power-of-progressive-economics-the-clinton-years/

"a bigger percentage gain": Brooks Jackson, "Obama's Final Numbers," FactCheck, September 29, 2017.

"there was a surplus of $236 billion": Brooks Jackson, "The Budget and Deficit Under Clinton," FactCheck, February 3, 2008.

"The Obama Tax Plan Would Eliminate Hundreds of Thousands": William Beach et al., "Obama Tax Hikes: The Economic and Fiscal Effects," The Heritage Foundation, September 20, 2010.

"[We have] high unemployment because small businesses": "Hannity Falsely Equates 'Small Businesses' with Those Making Over $250 per Year," *Media Matters*, October 6, 2010.

"In fact, the economy netted": Jackson, "Obama's Final Numbers."

"A 2016 study by a respected": Emanuel Saez, "Taxing the Rich More: Preliminary Evidence from the 2013 Tax Increase," (working paper 22798, National Bureau of Economic Research, November 2016), doi: 10.3386/w22798

Case Study: The Minimum Wage: A Maximum Job Killer?

"High hourly wages mean nothing": "Textile Wage Opposed by Council" *The New York Times*, July 5, 1938.

"What profiteth the laborer": U.S. Department of Labor, Bureau of Labor Statistics, *Record of the Discussion Before the U.S. Congress of the FLSA of 1938*, 873, 915, 929 (statement of Rep. John McClellan).

"An increase of $0.25 per hour": Thomas Rustici, "A Public Choice View of the Minimum Wage," *Cato Journal*, 5, no. 1 (Spring/Summer 1985): 8.

"GOVERNOR VETOES $1.50 MINIMUM PAY": Murray Seeger, "Governor Vetoes $1.50 Minimum Pay; New Bill Is Likely; Rockefeller Declares Rise Would Drive Out Industry and Cause Loss of Jobs; Labor Plea Rejected; Zaretzki Says Democrats Lack Votes to Override—$1.40 Measure Weighed," *The New York Times*, April 17, 1965.

"If the minimum wage were increased": Fair Labor Standards Amendments of 1977 (S. 1871), Hearings Before the Subcommittee on Labor of the Senate Committee of Human Resources, 95 Cong. (August 2, 1977), 170 (statements of Robert T. Thompson, Louis P. Neeb, and Jack Carlson, U.S. Chamber of Commerce).

"I am vitally concerned about the thousands": H.R. 3744, 95 Cong. Rec., H12268 (April 26, 1977) (statement of Rep. Eldon Rudd).

"The consequences of minimum wage laws": Milton Friedman, televised interview, 1970s (exact date unknown), youtube.com/watch?v=ca8Z__o52sk&ab_channel=amagilly. Link found via Mark. J Perry, "New Research Confirms That the Cruel Minimum Wage Law Has the Greatest Adverse Effects on the Most Vulnerable Workers," American Enterprise Institute, May 4, 2020.

"The minimum wage has caused more misery": William Finnegan, "Demonizing the Minimum Wage," *The New Yorker*, September 17, 2014.

"Those at greatest risk from a higher minimum": "The Right Minimum Wage: $0," *The New York Times*, January 14, 1987.

"Work is what low income people really need": 101 Cong. Rec. H2531 (June 14, 1989) (statement of Rep. Robert Walker).

"Now, what is the effect of this law?": 110 Cong. Rec. H264 (January 10, 2007) (statement of Rep. Jeb Hensarling).

"The federal minimum wage was last raised": Aimee Picchi, "It's Been a Record 11 Years Since the Last Increase in U.S. Minimum Wage," CBSNews.com, July 24, 2020.

"The wage is now worth 21 percent less": Ben Zipperer, "The Minimum Wage Has Lost 21% of Its Value Since Congress Last Raised the Wage," Economic Policy Institute, July 22, 2021.

"Look, I wish we could just pass a law": Pat Garofalo, "Top Republicans Oppose Obama's Call to Raise the Minimum Wage," Da, February 13, 2013.

"In fact, the impact of minimum wage usually": Steve Benen, "Rubio Takes a Stand Against a Minimum Wage," MSNBC.com, February 16, 2013.

"reshaping the academic consensus": "What Harm Do Minimum Wages Do?" *The Economist*, August 15, 2020.

"In 1993, when economists David Card and Alan Krueger": Card and Krueger, "Minimum Wages and Employment."

"one Nobel Prize winning economist": "Quotation of the Day: James Buchanan on the Minimum Wage," American Enterprise Institute, January 11, 2013.

"High New Jersey Minimum Wage Doesn't Seem to Deter": Sylvia Nasar, "High New Jersey Minimum Wage Doesn't Seem to Deter Fast-Food Hiring, Study Finds," *The New York Times*, May 20, 1993.

"analyzed data from all 22 increases": Paul K. Sonn and Yannet M. Lathrop, "Raise Wages, Kill Jobs?" National Employment Law Project, May 2016.

"But perhaps the most comprehensive recent analysis": Doruk Cengiz et al., "The Effect of Minimum Wages on Low-Wage Jobs," *Quarterly Journal of Economics*, 134, no. 3 (2019): 1405–1454, doi:10.1093/qje/qjz014

"Card was awarded the 2021 Nobel Prize in Economics": Nobel Prize Outreach, "David Card Facts," 2021, www.nobelprize.org/prizes/economic-sciences/2021/card/facts/

Seattle's Minimum Wage

"a growing number of states and localities have": Economic Policy Institute, "Minimum Wage Tracker," www.epi.org/minimum-wage-tracker

"In 2014, a coalition of labor and community leaders": Gregory Wallace, "Seattle Approves $15 Minimum Wage," CNN Business, June 3, 2014.

"You'll see businesses moving or not forming": Lynn Thompson and Amy Martinez, "Mayor's Plan Lifts Minimum Wage to $15—Eventually," *The Seattle Times*, May 2, 2014.

"They're [small businesses] the most likely to fail": Thompson and Martinez, "Mayor's Plan Lifts Minimum Wage to $15."

"Every [restaurant] operator I'm talking to": Sara Jones, "Why Are So Many Seattle Restaurants Closing Lately?" *Seattle Magazine*, November 27, 2018.

"As the implementation date for Seattle's": "Seattle's $15 Wage Law a Factor in Restaurant Closings," Washington Policy Center, March 11, 2015.

"A rigorous 2017 study": Michael Reich, Sylvia Allegretto, and Anna Godoey, "Seattle's Minimum Wage Experience, 2015–2016," Center on Wage and Employment Dynamics, University of California, Berkeley, June 2017.

"the same researchers in 2018": Allegretto et al., "The New Wave of Local Minimum Wage Policies."

"was ultimately moved to write a mea culpa": Jacob Vigdor, "The Minimum Wage Is a Lousy Anti-Poverty Program," *The Perfect and the Free* (blog), January 2, 2019.

"By 2017 the number of restaurants": Bethany Jean Clement, "Seattle's Crazy Restaurant Boom," *The Seattle Times*, January 16, 2017.

"A 10-year chart": Federal Reserve Bank of St. Louis, "All Employees: Leisure and Hospitality: Food Services and Drinking Places in Seattle-Tacoma-Bellevue, WA," fred.stlouisfed.org/graph

"King County, WA was consistently": U.S. Bureau of Labor Statistics, "Quarterly Census of Employment and Wages," www.bls.gov/cew

5: You'll Only Make It Worse

"The federal government declared war on poverty": Reagan, "State of the Union" (January 25, 1988).

"More than 20, persons were degraded": Michael Katz, *In the Shadow of the Poorhouse: A Social History of Welfare in America* (New York: Basic Books, 1996).

"The idle will beg in preference to working": Seth Rockman, *Welfare Reform in the Early Republic: A Brief History with Documents* (Long Grove, IL: Waveland Press, 2003), 127.

"[Unemployment Insurance] would increase unemployment": *Hearings on Unemployment Insurance, House Committee on Ways and Means*, 73 Cong. (March 21–24, 26–30, 1934) (statement of John Donnelly, Executive Vice President Illinois Association of Manufacturers).

"Now I don't want to sound unnecessarily coldhearted": Larry Kudlow, "More Unemployment Benefits Will Backfire," CNBC.com, October 5, 2009.

"But where will employers obtain the money": United States Senate, *Fair Labor Standards Amendments of 1971, Hearings Before the Subcommittee on Labor of the Committee on Labor and Public Welfare*, 92 Cong., 1st Sess. on S. 1861 and S. 2259 (May 26 and June 3, 8, 9, 10, 17, and 22, 1971), 269.

"Under these inflationary pressures": H.R. 3744, 95 Cong. Rec. H12268 (1977) (statement of Rep. Mickey Edwards).

"I've often said that the minimum-wage rate": "The Playboy Interview: Milton Friedman," *Playboy*, 20, no. 2 (February 1973), 51–68, 74.

"When we pass minimum wage legislation it says one thing": 101 Cong. Rec., H7765 (1989) (statement of Rep. Bob McEwen).

"This is an unemployment act that hurts minority youth": Jerold Waltman, *The Politics of the Minimum Wage* (Urbana-Champaign: University of Illinois Press, 2), 101.

"I understand it is called a minimum wage bill": Waltman, *The Politics of the Minimum Wage*, 101.

"Minimum wage laws may very well be": Michael D. LaFaive, "Minimum Wage and Fairness: in a Free-Market Economy, Wouldn't Employees Be Paid Less Than the Minimum Wage?" Mackinac Center for Public Policy, November 1, 1997.

"$15 minimum wage hurts workers": "$15 Minimum Wage Hurts Workers Who Need Help the Most," *Bloomberg Opinion*, July 9, 2019.

"Minimum Wage Rise Called Dangerous": "Minimum Wage Rise Called Dangerous; NAM [National Association of Manufacturers] Tells House Group It Would Cost $15 . . . in Higher Taxes and Prices," *The New York Times*, October 23, 1945.

"The problem with this left-wing economic engineering": Craig Harrington, "On Fox, Expansion of Overtime Protections Is

'Left-Wing Economic Engineering,'" *Media Matters*, June 10, 2015.

"[Medicare] could destroy private initiative": 113 Cong. Rec. S7018–S71029 159, no. 132, (September 30, 2013) (statement of Sen. Harry Reid, quoting Sen. Milward Simpson from a July 8, 1965 Medicare debate).

"President Bill Clinton's 1993 budget was ultimately credited": Suzy Khimm, "Obama Credits Clinton for the Boom Times of the 90s. Is He Right?" *The Washington Post*, August 6, 2012.

"The impact on job creation is going to be devastating": "Party Representatives Disagree on Deficit Reduction," CNN, August 2, 1993.

"at least two large Covid relief packages": Rachel Cohrs, "Trump Signs Second Major Covid Relief Package," *Modern Healthcare*, March 18, 2020.

"For decades, the Left has been pushing": Alli Flick, "How Unemployment Benefits Have Become the New Welfare and How to Fix It," the Foundation for Government Accountability, August 2, 2021.

"By late August of 2021, twenty-six of them had taken steps": Greg Iacurci, "26 States Ended Federal Unemployment Benefits Early. Data Suggest It's Not Getting People Back to Work," CNBC.com, August 4, 2021.

"As Ronald Reagan once said": Sean Murphy, "Oklahoma Governor Announces End to Extra Unemployment Money," *Associated Press*, May 17, 2021.

"U.S. Chamber of Commerce Wants End to $300": Nicholas Reimann, "U.S. Chamber of Commerce Wants End to $300-a-Week Federal Unemployment Benefits—Blames It on Bad Jobs Report," *Forbes*, May 7, 2021.

"Unemployment Benefits Forever?": Editorial Board, "Unemployment Benefits Forever? Treasury Suggests How States Can Continue the Incentives Not to Work," *Wall Street Journal*, August 20, 2021.

"It's not fair to the people": Emma Hurt, "Georgia to Cut Jobless Benefits to Push People to Work," *Associated Press*, May 13, 2021.

"Cutting off Jobless Benefits Is Found": Ben Casselman, "Cutting off Jobless Benefits Is Found to Get Few Back to Work; Prematurely Ending Federal Programs Has Little Effect on Employment but Sharply Cut Spending, Potentially Hurting State Economies, Researchers Say," *The New York Times*, August 20, 2021.

"Labor Department numbers showed" Casselman, "Cutting off Jobless Benefits."

"A separate study by well-regarded economists looked at 19 states": Kyle Coombs et al., "Early Withdrawal of Pandemic Unemployment Insurance: Effects on Earnings, Employment and Consumption" (working paper, Opportunity Insights, August 20, 2021), files.michaelstepner.com/pandemicUIexpiration-paper.pdf

"Census Bureau figures show": Heather Long and Amy Goldstein, "Poverty Fell Overall in 2020 as a Result of Massive Stimulus Checks and Unemployment Aid, Census Bureau Says," *The Washington Post*, September 14, 2021.

"Another study found that child poverty plummeted": Jason DeParle, "Pandemic Aid Programs Spur a Record Drop in Poverty," *The New York Times*, July 28, 2021.

Case Study: The Welfare Debate

"By taxing the good people to pay": Katz, *In the Shadow of the Poorhouse.*

"Welfare also plays a powerful role": Patrick Fagan and Robert Rector, "How Welfare Harms Kids," The Heritage Foundation, June 5, 1996.

"Policies that increase dependency": President Ronald Reagan, "Address Before a Joint Session of the Congress on the State of the Union" (February 6, 1985), The American Presidency Project, https://www.presidency.ucsb.edu/documents/address -before-joint-session-the-congress-the-state-the-union-5

"President Vetoes Child Care Plan": Jack Rosenthal, "President Vetoes Child Care Plan as Irresponsible; He Terms Bill Unworkable and Voices Fear It Would Weaken Role of Family; Congress Fight Vowed but Overriding of Nixon's Step Is Doubted," *The New York Times*, December 10, 1971.

"1996 welfare reform bill": Rebecca Vallas and Jeremy Slevin, "Everything You Wanted to Know About the 1996 Welfare Law but Were Afraid to Ask," Center for American Progress, August 22, 2016, talkpoverty.org/2016/08/22/everything-wanted-know-1996-welfare-law-afraid-ask

"The sometimes-liberal New Republic": Joshua Holland, "Why Americans Hate Welfare," BillMoyers.com, March 6, 2014.

"With a cover photo": Image: *"New Republic* Day of Reckoning," BillMoyers.com, March 2014, billmoyers.com/wp-content /uploads/2014/03/TNR-welfare.jpg

"One authoritative 2018 Stanford study of studies": Robert Moffitt and Stephanie Garlow, "Did Welfare Reform Increase Employment and Reduce Poverty?" *Pathways: A Magazine on Poverty, Inequality, and Social Policy* (Winter 2018): 17–21.

"In 1997, the year": Gretchen Livingston, "About One-Third of U.S. Children Are Living with an Unmarried Parent," Pew Research Center, April 27, 2018.

"We don't want to turn the safety net into a hammock": Arthur Delaney and Michael McAuliff, "Paul Ryan Wants 'Welfare Reform Round 2,'" *HuffPost*, March 20, 2012.

"Concern for the poor is often equated": Daren Bakst and Patrick Tyrrell, "Big Government Policies That Hurt the Poor and How to Address Them," The Heritage Foundation, April 5, 2017.

"access to food stamps in childhood leads to": Hilary W. Hoynes, Diane Whitmore Schanzenbach, and Douglas Almond, "Long-Run Impacts of Childhood Access to the Safety Net," (working paper 18535, National Bureau of Economic Research, November 2012), doi: 10.3386/w18535

"Getting people off of welfare into a productive job": Stephen Moore, "Welfare Is the New Work," *The Washington Times*, July 31, 2016.

Oh, Those Unintended Consequences

"We cannot get rid of slavery": Thomas Dew, "Text of the Pro-Slavery Argument (1832)," Dictionary of American History, www.encyclopedia.com/history/dictionaries-thesauruses -pictures-and-press-releases/text-pro-slavery-argument -1832-thomas-dew

"Women's participation in political life": William Loren Katz and Laurie R. Lehman, *The Cruel Years: American Voices at the Dawn of the Twentieth Century* (Boston: Beacon Press, 2003), 25–26.

"Confiscation of private wealth": "Confiscation of Wealth."

"Recycling itself can cause environmental harm": Lynn Scarlett, "A Consumer's Guide to Environmental Myths and Realities," The Reason Foundation and The National Center for Policy Analysis, 1991.

"The net result could well be a greater probability of oil spills": "Shipowners Call Oil Pollution Act a Big Mistake," *The Journal of Commerce*, October 22, 1990.

"The more efficient new cars won't save": "Automakers Oppose Law-Mileage Penalties," *The Chicago Tribune*, June 29, 1975.

"If our manufacturers leave": "California Lawmakers Reach Emissions Deal," *Greenwire*, August 31, 2006.

"If you're sticking your head in the sand": Manu Raju, "Joe Manchin Says He's 'Very Very' Disturbed About Reconciliation Proposals on Climate Change," CNN.com, July 15, 2021.

6: It's Socialism!

"Isn't this socialism?": Robin Toner, "New Deal Debate for a New Era," *The New York Times*, August 1, 2007.

"Evil empire": Editors, "This Day in History [March 08, 1983]: Reagan Refers to U.S.S.R as 'Evil Empire' Again," History.com, www.history.com/this-day-in-history/reagan-refers-to-u-s-s-r-as-evil-empire-again

"They attacked a modest": Rachael Bade et al., "POLITICO Playbook: Grisham Dishes on Melania," *POLITICO*, September 13, 2021.

"In 1984, during an economic depression": Andrew Glass, "Congress Enacts an Income Tax Law, Aug. 28, 1894," *POLITICO*, August 28, 2018.

"It may be impracticable": "Women's Suffrage and Other Visions of Right-Wing Apocalypse."

"[This tax is based on] principles as communistic": Steven R. Weisman, *The Great Tax Wars* (New York: Simon & Schuster, 2004), 151.

"The fury of ignorant class hatred": Weisman, *The Great Tax Wars*, 160.

"President Teddy Roosevelt proposed": Susan Dunn, "Teddy Roosevelt Betrayed," *The New York Times*, August 9, 1999.

"[The tax gave] more encouragement to state socialism": Weisman, *The Great Tax Wars*, 201.

"[Taxing the rich] was supported by the Socialist party": Weisman, *The Great Tax Wars*, 225.

"Signed the 1913 Revenue Act": Scott Bomboy, "How We Wound Up with the Income Tax," National Constitution Center, February 3, 2021.

"Estate taxes, carried to an excess, in no way differ": Andrew William Mellon, *Taxation: The People's Business* (New York: Macmillan, 1924), 122.

"I do not believe that the Government should seek": "Reform in Government Taxation Methods," *Commercial West*, 48 (August 1, 1925): 21.

"The estate tax is communistic in essence": "The Federal Estate Tax," *The Washington Post*, February 7, 1926.

"[A measure restricting child labor] would mean the destruction": Chaim Rosenberg, *Child Labor in America: A History* (Jefferson, NC: McFarland, 2013), 187.

"DR. BUTLER ASSAILS CHILD LABOR BILL": "Dr. Butler Assails Child Labor Bill; Proposed Amendment Would Imperil Home, School, Church and Nation, He Says," *The New York Times*, February 3, 1934.

"[Child labor laws are] a communistic effort to nationalize": Sherrod Brown, *Desk 88: Eight Progressive Senators Who Changed America* (New York: Farrar, Straus, and Giroux, 2019).

"The New Deal is now undisguised state socialism": Sean Wilentz, "Fighting Words," *Democracy Journal*, 48 (Spring 2018).

"Frankly the NLRA impresses me as having been written": U.S. Senate, *To Create A National Labor Board, Hearings before the Committee on Education and Labor*, 73 Cong. (March 27, 1934).

"The end of democracy": Michael Parrish, "New Deal Critics," Bill of Rights Institute, billofrightsinstitute.org/essays/new-deal-critics

"The lash of the dictator will be felt": Matt Miller, "Matt Miller: Déjà Vu on Obamacare," *The Washington Post*, October 30, 2013.

"Too long have we introduced carelessly": "Denounces Spread of Federal Power," *The New York Times*, April 28, 1936.

"Social security right now is a collectivist system": Vincent J. Miller, "Secret Ryan Transcript: Social Security and Medicare are the Target," *America Magazine*, September 19, 2012.

"This would be communism with a vengeance": "The Fantasy of the Living Wage," *Nation's Business*, 11 (June 1923), 16–18.

"No greater calamity could befall the wage earners": Alice Kessler-Harris, *A Woman's Wage: Historical Meanings and Social Consequences* (Lexington: University Press of Kentucky: 1991), 50.

"[It] will destroy small industry": Stephen W. Stathis, *Landmark Debates in Congress: From the Declaration of Independence to the War in Iraq* (Washington, DC: CQ Press, 2008), 323.

"[The Fair Labor Standards Act] constitutes a step": "Women's Suffrage and Other Visions of Right-Wing Apocalypse."

"VANDENBERG FEARS 'FASCIST' WAGE BILL": "Vandenberg Fears 'Fascist' Wage Bill," *The New York Times*, June 6, 1937.

"[It] will lead to compulsory arbitration": "Vandenberg Fears 'Fascist' Wage Bill."

"[T]he Federal wage and hour law is one of the most vicious": "Letter to the President of the National Federation of Independent Businesses from Lewis Manufacturing Co., February 24, 1960," in U.S. House of Representatives, *Hearings Before Subcommittee on Labor-Management Relations of the Committee on Education and Labor,* 86th Cong., 2d Sess., (February 16–29, 1960).

"The creeping socialism begins": Sylvia Nasar, "High New Jersey Minimum Wage Doesn't Seem to Deter Fast-Food Hiring, Study Finds," *The New York Times*, May 20, 1993.

"Slowly but surely they're taking away your liberty": Peter T. Kilborn, "A Minimum-Impact Minimum Wage," *The New York Times*, April 6, 1997.

"These 'four horsemen' of racial agitation": "Mississippi Gov Alleges MLK Communist 1963, Washington, USA," *Associated Press*, July 12, 1963, shutterstock.com/editorial/image-editorial/mississippi-gov-alleges-mlk-communist-1963-washington-usa-6639245a.

"[There is a] Communist conspiracy": "Eastland Labels Rights Drive 'Red'; Sees a Hoax in Mississippi Disappearance of 3 Men," *The New York Times*, July 23, 1964.

"EASTLAND LABELS RIGHTS DRIVE 'RED'": "Eastland Labels Rights Drive 'Red.'"

"Galloping socialism in its purest form": Curtis Seltzer, *Fire in the Hole: Miners and Managers in the American Coal Industry* (Lexington: University Press of Kentucky, 1985), 99.

"The Act broadly authorizes the Secretary": "Life or Death for Your Business?" *Nation's Business*, April 1968, in *Occupational Health and Safety Act of 1968: Hearings Before the Subcommittee on Labor of the Committee on Labor and Public Welfare*, 90th Cong., 2d Sess. on S. 2864 (February 15, June 12, 19, 24, 28, and July 2, 1968).

"There is no evidence": *Occupational Health and Safety Act of 1968: Hearings Before the Subcommittee on Labor of the Committee on Labor and Public Welfare*, 90th Cong., 2d Sess. on S. 2864 (June 12, 1968) (statement of Wallace Smith).

"Pat Buchanan warned": Nancy L. Cohen, "Why America Never Had Universal Child Care," *The New Republic*, April 23, 2013.

"The CDA would commit the vast moral authority": Jack Rosenthal, "President Vetoes Child Care Plan as Irresponsible," *The New York Times*, December 10, 1971.

"This disturbing trend": Peter Dreier and Donald Cohen, "Why Did CNN's Dana Bash 'Cry Wolf' About Paid Family Leave? Is She Working for the Chamber of Commerce?" *HuffPost*, October 14, 2015.

"America's business owners are a resilient bunch": Cristina Marcos, "GOP Pans Push for Paid Leave," *The Hill*, January 22, 2015.

"This socialist diktat takes feel-good politics": Donald Cohen, "Chamber of Commerce Was Wrong About Family and Medical Leave Law," *HuffPost*, February 4, 2013.

"This socialist diktat takes feel-good politics to a new level": Steve Lonegan, "Paid Family Leave Measure Is Just Another Scam," *Bergen Record*.

Our Socialist Presidents

"Roosevelt is a socialist": Angie Drobnic Holan, "FDR Was Called a Socialist and a Communist," Politifact.com, September 22, 2009.

"[President Harry Truman's policies] would commit us" and "BYRD TIES TRUMAN TO SOCIALIST DRIFT": "Byrd Ties Truman to Socialist Drift; Tells Political Scientists That Policies Sap Free Enterprise to Point of 'No Retreat,'" *The New York Times*, April 27, 1950.

"Mr. President, because of your socialist tendencies": William Manchester, *The Death of a President: November 1963* (New York: Harper & Row, 1967), 128.

"It is . . . incredible to try to understand": Ian Millhiser, "A Brief, 90-Year History of Republicans Calling Democrats 'Socialists,'" ThinkProgress, March 6, 2019.

"[Johnson's Great Society program came] close enough": Fred Siegel, "The Forgotten Failures of the Great Society," *National Review*, January 9, 2020.

"[If Carter is elected] what happens": Clare Booth Luce, "The Light at the End of the Tunnel of Love: Jimmy Carter's Christian Socialism," *National Review*, November 12, 1976 (republished February 13, 2020).

"The man is a socialist": John E. Becker, "Socialist—Is Bill Clinton a Socialist?" *John Becker for Ohio*, October 13, 1993, www.beckergop.com/1993/10/13/socialist-is-bill-clinton-a-socialist-october-13-1993/

"Obama's a hardcore socialist": Sarah Owen, "David Koch Gives President Obama Zero Credit for Bin Laden's Death," *New York Magazine*, May 5, 2011.

"Don't ask me to get inside the mind": Bill Glauber, "Ron Johnson Called Joe Biden 'a Liberal, Progressive, Socialist, Marxist.' Can Someone Be All Those Things?" *Milwaukee Journal Sentinel*, June 11, 2021.

"The $3.5 billion Biden plan": Jonathan Chait, "Marco Rubio Doesn't Know What a 'Socialist' Is, But He Knows Biden Is One," *New York Magazine*, October 8, 2021.

"[Biden's Build Back Better plan is] meant to be a Trojan horse": Mitch McConnell, "Democrats' Reckless Taxing and Spending Spree Designed to Reduce Employment and Undermine Work," *Kentucky New Era*, October 28, 2021, www.kentuckynewera.com/multimedia/video/news/video_ec814c97-bb18-545d-81fa-035da713cde5.html

"I beat the socialist": Oma Seddiq, "'I Beat the Socialist': Biden Reminds Voters 'Worried About Socialism' That He Won the Party Nomination, Not Bernie Sanders," *Insider*, September 22, 2020.

"Referring to Sen. Bernie Sanders": Linda Qui, "Bernie Sanders—Socialist or Democratic Socialist?" PolitiFact.com, August 23, 2015.

"*Socialism is what they called*": U.S. National Archives, Harry S. Truman Library and Museum, "Rear Platform and Other Informal Remarks in New York," October 10, 1952, www.trumanlibrary.gov/library/public-papers/289/rear-platform-and-other-informal-remarks-new-york

Case Study: Healthcare

"*Costs approximately twice as much . . . with worse health outcomes*": Nisha Kurani and Cynthia Cox, "What Drives Health Spending in the U.S. Compared to Other Countries," *Health System Tracker*, September 25, 2020.

"*The association has for years been a foe*" and "*DOCTORS MEET ON 'PERIL' IN SECURITY PLANS*": "Doctors Meet on 'Peril' in Security Plans; Illness Insurance Moves Stir Profession," *The New York Times*, February 15, 1935.

"*I considered it socialism*": Paul Starr, *The Social Transformation of American Medicine* (New York: Basic Books, 1982), 283.

"*Would socialized medicine lead to socialization of other phases*": Starr, *The Social Transformation of American Medicine*, 284–285.

"*[If Medicare legislation passes,] we will awake*": Ronald Reagan Presidential Foundation, "Ronald Reagan Speaks Out on Socialized Medicine—Audio," YouTube, July 23, 2009, youtube.com/watch?v=AYrlDlrLDSQ&ab_channel=ReaganFoundation.

Reagan LP Cover: Wikipedia, "Ronald Reagan Speaks Out Against Socialized Medicine," last modified January 26, 2021, en.wikipedia.org/wiki/Ronald_Reagan_Speaks_Out_Against_Socialized_Medicine#/media/File:Reagan-LPcover.jpg.

"*A.M.A. CRITICIZES MEDICARE IN AD*": "AMA Criticizes Medicare in Ad; Says It Would Be 'Beginning of Socialized Medicine'" *The New York Times*, June 9, 1965.

"*Realize that the doctor's fight against socialized medicine*": Ron-

ald Reagan, *The Greatest Speeches of Ronald Reagan*, 2nd ed. (New York: Humanix Books, 2003), 3.

"*It is socialism*": "Women's Suffrage and Other Visions of Right-Wing Apocalypse."

"*Some people think that people are entitled to health care*": Richard D. Lyons, "Chamber Seeking Doctor Members," *The New York Times*, October 14, 1971.

"*[Clinton's health-care proposal] resembles long-standing plans*": "Clinton's Prescription," *The Orange County Register*, September 28, 1992.

"*We have arrived at socialized medicine*": Robert J. Samuelson, "Socialized Medicine in America," *The Washington Post*, September 29, 1993.

"*[The Clintons' health care initiative is] washed-over old-time bureaucratic liberalism*": Robert Pear, "For Mrs. Clinton, Health Plan Left Lessons and Questions," *The New York Times*, October 21, 2.

"*The last thing we need is Hillarycare*": Liz Marlantes and Mary Walsh, "Hillary Clinton: Health Care 'Déjà Vu All Over Again'," ABCNews.com, September 17, 2007.

"*When you hear Democrats in particular talk*": Paul Steinhauser, "Giuliani Attacks Democratic Health Plans as 'Socialist'," CNN Politics, July 31, 2007.

"*[The GOP] must decide soon where they stand*": "Report: Limbaugh Conservatives Continue 75-Year-Old "Socialized Medicine" Smear," *Media Matters*, March 5, 2009.

"*[I am] confident that Congress will pass the Kennedy-Hatch KidCare bill*": Phyllis Schlafly, "NEA Convention Delegates Gather to Gloat," *Eagle Forum*, July 23, 1997.

"*The Children's Health Insurance Program has given Democrats*": Robert Pear, "Expanded Health Program for Children Causes Clash," *The New York Times*, April 1, 2007.

"[The Democrats'] vision for the future: socialized medicine": Robert Pear, "House Passes Children's Health Plan 225–204," *The New York Times*, August 2, 2007.

"Ask why Barack Obama wants to make us all wards of the state": Lisa Schiffren, "Take This and Run," *National Review*, October 6, 2008.

"This will increase burdens on taxpayers": Sean Lengell, "Children's Health Bill Clears Senate," *The Washington Times*, January 30, 2009.

"This is the crown jewel of socialism": Brian Lambert, "Obamacare Is 'Crown Jewel of Socialism,' Says Bachmann," *MinnPost*, January 20, 2011.

"We are treading dangerously close to bureaucratic intervention": "Fleming Rips Obama's Budget Plan," KTBS.com, February 26, 2009.

"[The healthcare bill is a] headlong rush into socialism: Eric Zimmermann, "Steele Denounces Healthcare as 'Socialist Utopia,'" *The Hill*, March 18, 2010.

"Nearly 18 million": Matt Broaddus and Aviva Aron-Dine, "Uninsured Rate Rose Again in 2019, Further Eroding Earlier Progress," Center on Budget and Policy Priorities, September 15, 2020.

"Obamacare Will Suck the Life Out of the Economy": Edward Morrissey, "Obamacare Will Suck the Life Out of the Economy," CNBC, June 26, 2014.

"Obamacare brings record low": Dan Mangan, "Obamacare Brings Record Low for U.S. Health Uninsured Rate," CNBC, May 17, 2016.

ABOUT THE AUTHORS

Nick Hanauer is an entrepreneur and a venture capitalist, the founder of the public policy incubator Civic Ventures, and the host of the podcast *Pitchfork Economics*. He lives in Seattle.

Joan Walsh is national affairs correspondent for *The Nation* magazine and the co-producer of the Emmy-nominated documentary *The Sit-In: Harry Belafonte Hosts The Tonight Show.* She lives in New York.

Donald Cohen is the founder and executive director of the research and policy center In the Public Interest and co-author of *The Privatization of Everything* (The New Press). He lives in Los Angeles.

PUBLISHING IN THE PUBLIC INTEREST

Thank you for reading this book published by The New Press. The New Press is a nonprofit, public interest publisher. New Press books and authors play a crucial role in sparking conversations about the key political and social issues of our day.

We hope you enjoyed this book and that you will stay in touch with The New Press. Here are a few ways to stay up to date with our books, events, and the issues we cover:

- Sign up at www.thenewpress.com/subscribe to receive updates on New Press authors and issues and to be notified about local events
- www.facebook.com/newpressbooks
- www.twitter.com/thenewpress
- www.instagram.com/thenewpress

Please consider buying New Press books for yourself; for friends and family; or to donate to schools, libraries, community centers, prison libraries, and other organizations involved with the issues our authors write about.

The New Press is a 501(c)(3) nonprofit organization. You can also support our work with a tax-deductible gift by visiting www.thenewpress.com/donate.